James Ross is Senio̶r̶ ̶̶̶̶̶̶ ̶i̶n̶ ̶L̶a̶t̶e̶ ̶M̶e̶d̶i̶e̶v̶a̶l̶ History at the University of Winchester. He has published extensively on late medieval England, its politics and government, and is the author of *John de Vere, Thirteenth Earl of Oxford, 1442–1513: 'The Foremost Man of the Kingdom'*.

JAMES ROSS

Henry VI

A Good, Simple and Innocent Man

PENGUIN BOOKS

PENGUIN BOOKS

UK | USA | Canada | Ireland | Australia
India | New Zealand | South Africa

Penguin Books is part of the Penguin Random House group of companies
whose addresses can be found at global.penguinrandomhouse.com

First published by Allen Lane 2016
First published in Penguin Books 2019
001

Set in 9.5/13.5 pt Sabon LT Std
Typeset by Jouve (UK), Milton Keynes
Printed and bound in Great Britain by Clays Ltd, Elcograf S.p.A.

ISBN: 978–0–241–38041–3

www.greenpenguin.co.uk

Contents

For A. C.

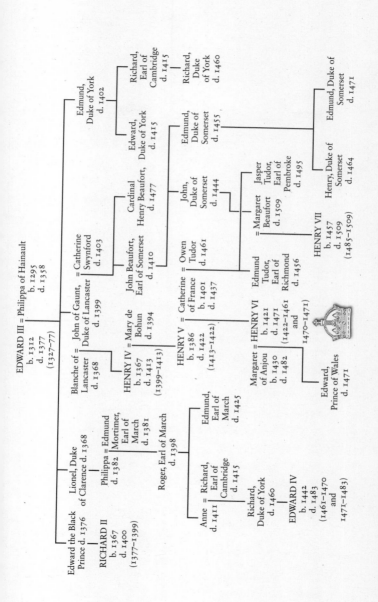

EDWARD III = Philippa of Hainault
b. 1312   b. 1295
d. 1377   d. 1358
(1327-77)

Edward the Black
Prince d. 1376

RICHARD II
b. 1367
d. 1400
(1377-1399)

Lionel, Duke
of Clarence d. 1368

Philippa = Edmund
d. 1382   Mortimer, Earl
of March
d. 1381

Roger, Earl of March
d. 1398

Edmund, Earl
of March
d. 1425

Anne = Richard, Earl
d. 1411   of Cambridge
d. 1415

Richard,
Duke of York
d. 1460

EDWARD IV
b. 1442
d. 1483
(1461-1470 and
1471-1483)

Blanche of = John of Gaunt, = Catherine
Lancaster   Duke of Lancaster   Swynford
d. 1368   d. 1399   d. 1403

HENRY IV = Mary de
b. 1367   Bohun
d. 1413   d. 1394
(1399-1413)

HENRY V = Catherine
b. 1386   of France
d. 1422   b. 1401
(1413-1422)   d. 1437

Margaret = HENRY VI
of Anjou   b. 1421
b. 1430   d. 1471
d. 1482   (1422-1461 and
1470-1471)

Edward,
Prince of Wales
d. 1471

John Beaufort,
Earl of Somerset
d. 1410

John,
Duke of Somerset
d. 1444

Cardinal
Henry Beaufort,
d. 1477

Owen = Catherine
Tudor   of France
d. 1461   b. 1401
d. 1437

Edmund
Tudor, Earl of
Richmond
d. 1456

= Margaret
Beaufort
d. 1509

HENRY VII
b. 1457
d. 1509
(1485-1509)

Jasper
Tudor, Earl of
Pembroke
d. 1495

Edmund,
Duke of York
d. 1402

Edward,
Duke of York
d. 1415

Richard,
Earl of
Cambridge
d. 1415

Richard,
Duke
of York
d. 1460

Edmund,
Duke of Somerset
d. 1455

Henry, Duke of
Somerset
d. 1464

Edmund, Duke of
Somerset
d. 1471

Henry VI

Introduction
The Enigma of Henry VI

Few would disagree that Henry VI, son of Henry V and last king of the house of Lancaster, was one of the least able and least successful kings ever to rule England, although people continue to disagree, as they did during Henry VI's reign itself, about how and why this should have been so. Shakespeare, writing his history plays 150 years later, described Henry's England as a state of which 'so many had the managing, / That they lost France and made his England bleed'. The great playwright thus neatly encapsulated the disasters of the loss of Henry V's French conquest and the outbreak of the Wars of the Roses in the last few years of Henry VI's reign, while emphasizing the common perception that Henry was dominated by the personalities around him.[1] Shakespeare was not incorrect, but both the king and his reign were considerably more complex.

Within a few years of Henry VI's final deposition from the English throne in 1471, two writers were confronting his legacy. Sir John Fortescue, one of England's chief justices, the Lancastrian loyalist who disavowed his writings when he made his peace with Henry's Yorkist successor, King Edward IV, wrote a tract suggesting reforms to the monarchy, known today as the *Governance of England*, shortly after 1471 as Edward IV, finally secure on his throne, began to rule in his own style. While not explicitly referring to Henry VI's failings, many of Fortescue's political solutions were to problems caused by them, at least in part – most notably Henry's excessive, open-handed generosity, one of the leitmotivs of his reign. Fortescue argued that a king should be restricted in what lands and revenues he could alienate or grant away from the crown estates; trying to square the circle, he argued, not very convincingly, that 'this may in nothing restrain the King's power. For it is no power to more alienate and put away; but it is power to more have and keep to himself.'[2] In other words, Fortescue argued that, in restricting the king's power to impoverish himself, the king would become more powerful. Fortescue's advice, cogent though it was, did not noticeably change Edward's style of kingship, though some of his ideas perhaps influenced Henry VI's nephew, Henry Tudor, when he took the throne in 1485.

Another contemporary of Henry VI, John Blacman, a fellow of Eton and Henry's former chaplain, wrote a detailed description of the king around a decade after his death. Blacman passed over the practical and conceptual problems of kingship that Henry's reign had thrown up, instead focusing on the king's personality and explaining his failings as an earthly monarch by implying that he led an exemplary religious life that was more in keeping with sainthood than kingship – a picture that historians through the ages have been wary of accepting, given later, official, attempts to have Henry canonized as a saint. As these rather different attempts to understand him – Blacman's positive spin on his failings, Fortescue's suggested remedies for his errors – show, Henry VI was and remains an enigma.

There is of course a further issue. It is difficult enough for biographers to grasp the personality and character of great figures of the twentieth or twenty-first centuries, despite the comparative abundance of private letters, diaries, public speeches, broadcasts or written works, and contemporary comments. It is far more difficult for medieval historians to grasp the personality and character of those living five hundred years before, even that of a king. Private records revealing innermost thoughts are very rare, governmental records noted acts carried out in the king's name as a matter of course without necessarily revealing the agency behind them, contemporary comments were likely to be after the event and with an axe to grind, and an individual's acts, though providing hints as to his or her motivations, are subject to interpretation.

Even in this context, Henry VI's character and personality are particularly elusive. Not only was he, in the eyes of many contemporaries and historians, a passive, introverted figure, but even the surviving documentary evidence on Henry is peculiarly open to question. For few other kings would we question so closely, and with some justification, whether the words written in his name were his own, whether the documents he signed or the acts he made as king were his or were inspired, manipulated or dictated by those around him, his wife, his leading ministers or his courtiers and household servants. For almost no other medieval figure is the evidence so lacking in authority.

The nature of the evidence explains why there has been such a variety of views among modern historians on Henry's character. The most devastating view was that of one of the greatest of late-medieval historians, K. B. McFarlane, writing in the 1930s, for whom in Henry, 'second childhood succeeded first without the usual interval'.[3] This judgement was little questioned for almost half a century until Ralph Griffiths, in his monumental study of the reign, portrayed a king who made decisions, especially in the areas that interested him, but who left most of the government of the realm to others until his collapse in 1453, from which he was unlikely to have made a full recovery: Henry was 'well-meaning, but lacking in judgement'.[4] Griffiths's view has been influential, but in 1996 John Watts published a radical new interpretation of the king, much closer to McFarlane's, in which Henry was little more than a puppet, with no independent will, and all the acts of his reign were actually carried out in his name by those around the king – royal authority was thus an elaborate facade. While the argument is sophisticated and the conclusions on the political culture of English politics at the time are of great interest, Watts's view of Henry himself has not been accepted by many historians. Indeed, recent accounts of Henry have emphasized the evidence that shows Henry's active decision-making.[5]

Henry reigned for thirty-nine years until his deposition in 1461, was in exile or captivity for a further nine, and resumed his royal power in 1470 for seven months until his murder. He succeeded his father as king at only nine months, and the first half of his reign was dominated by the latter phases of the Hundred Years War, which finally ended in catastrophic defeat for the English in 1453. Conflict shifted from foreign war to civil war, while one faction then another sought to dominate the governance of England, as Henry failed to supply the requisite royal leadership to lead to successful war or domestic stability. Eventually he was dethroned by the first Yorkist king, Edward IV, after the bloody Battle of Towton in 1461. His cause seemed hopeless, especially after his capture and imprisonment in 1464, and was only revived by splits in the Yorkist regime, though Edward IV ended these with his victory at the Battle of Barnet in 1471; a few weeks later, Edward's victory at Tewkesbury saw Henry's son killed and his last chance to remain king ended. Henry was put to death in the Tower of London a few days later.

This book cannot hope to give a detailed analysis or narrative of the events of Henry's reign. Instead, the focus will be on Henry as a man and as a king: a biography of a man whose reign has been condemned as the 'nadir of the English monarchy',[6] and yet a man who was admired during his lifetime for his piety, and who perhaps would have been England's royal saint had Henry VIII not broken with the papacy after 1529. It will show an 'occasional' king; a man who could, on occasion, assert his royal will and make decisions, but whose interests were not those of most medieval kings, being far more focused on his afterlife than his actual life, whose faith, piety and spirituality were far more important to him than the administration, warfare and politics that comprised the essence of late-medieval kingship. His different priorities and only occasional engagement with the vital task of governance were directly, though not solely, responsible for the disasters that engulfed England during his reign.

I
Behind the Facade: Henry's Character and Capability

Henry was born at Windsor on 6 December, St Nicholas's day, in 1421, the only child of his father Henry V and his new queen, Catherine of France. Just nine months later, the baby boy acceded to the throne when his father died of dysentery contracted at the siege of Meaux. No Englishman had ever become king so early in life, nor had such a daunting inheritance. Few kings had ever been so respected as his father, Henry V, or so successful during their lifetimes: an intimidating role model for Henry VI to emulate. However, the military, political and economic practicalities he left behind were problematic. Henry V had effectively committed England to a long-term war in defence of his title as heir to the throne of France; but while he and his Burgundian allies controlled northern France, including Paris, most of the central and southern parts of the country remained committed to his Valois opponent, the Dauphin, shortly to become Charles VII of France. After Henry V's untimely death the English, ably led by the eldest of his two surviving brothers, John, Duke of Bedford, continued to advance until 1429, and then stabilized the military situation after the shock of defeat at the siege of Orléans and the emergence of Joan of Arc. Yet all this brought with it an understanding that the realization of Henry VI's claim to be King of France was bound to be a difficult process at best.

England itself remained stable enough during Henry VI's long minority. Political strife between Henry V's youngest brother, Humphrey, Duke of Gloucester, who expected to govern England during his nephew's young minority, and his uncle Cardinal Beaufort, who exercised a considerable amount of power as a result of his prodigious wealth and political ability, did not spill over into violence, and English martial energies were more or less committed to France. However, the latter part of Henry's minority also saw the beginning of a major economic slump, in part a result of a bullion shortage across Europe, which saw rents fall, but, more pressingly, overseas trade slump dramatically during the 1440s, greatly reducing the crown's income from customs duties, the biggest single contributor to the English Exchequer.

Henry VI's fitful engagement with these problems was some years in the future, but while we know a great deal about the warfare and politics of the years between 1422 and 1436 we know little of his early life. Henry's first years were spent in mainly female company; Elizabeth Ryman seems to have had command around the infant, with a principal nurse, Joan Asteley, and a day nurse, Matilda Fosbroke, his other constant companions. In 1424 Lady Alice Butler was appointed his governess to train him in courtesy, discipline and the other things required of a toddler who happened to be king, and had the power to administer reasonable chastisement as required. Henry's mother was also close at hand, residing, in part, in the royal household. As queen, she did not have such an immediate and important role in his upbringing as most modern mothers, and indeed was not always physically present, but nonetheless would have had very regular contact with her child. In 1428, the largely female company that had surrounded him was replaced by a largely male one. At this point, aged seven, Henry was deemed old enough to have a tutor, and Richard Beauchamp, Earl of Warwick, a paragon of chivalry and other manly virtues, was appointed to teach him 'good manners, letters, languages, nurture and courtesy', and, more importantly, to love, fear and honour God, embrace virtue and hate sin.[1] This latter element was catered for in part by the purchase of a primer, or religious manual, and within a year Henry could recite some of the services. Martial play was encouraged by the purchase of two little 'coat-armours' and 'eight swords ... some greater and some smaller, for to learn the king to play in his tender age'.[2]

Until 1429, Henry played little public role. He was present on the opening day of most parliaments of the 1420s, and on one or two other ceremonial occasions in London, but was largely secluded from affairs of government, moving between a small number of favoured royal residences in the south-east, such as Windsor, Eltham and Westminster. Henry's ceremonial and formal role began in earnest in 1429, at the age of eight. On Sunday, 6 November he was crowned King of England at Westminster in a gruelling set of ceremonies, comprising a morning procession from the Tower to show himself to his people, a public audience in Westminster Hall, the coronation itself in Westminster Abbey – including being anointed with the holy oil reportedly given to St Thomas Becket – and which also involved repeated prostrations, disrobings and prayers. This was followed by a huge banquet back in Westminster Hall. What effect the ceremony, specially adapted for Henry in his role as King of both England and France, and the banquet – which had a display with great emphasis on the royal saints of both kingdoms, Edward the Confessor and St Louis – had on the young king cannot be known. Nor can that of his French coronation two years later.

Leaving England in April 1430, Henry was at the Norman capital of Rouen for almost a year while the army that accompanied him stabilized the military situation in northern France caused by the unexpected reversal at the siege of Orléans in 1429 and by Joan of Arc, shining brightly but briefly, who had inspired a French military resurgence. Henry did not enter Paris until 2 December 1431, and was crowned on 16 December amid considerable pomp – not considerable enough, however, to impress at least one contemporary Parisian who complained about the English elements of the coronation service and the food, organized by the English authorities. Even the coronation in Paris was an acknowledgement of English failure, at least to some extent. French kings were traditionally crowned in Rheims, some ninety miles east of Paris, but that city had been captured by the French in the campaign of 1429. That Henry was not crowned at Rheims, where his maternal ancestors had been, is likely to have been a disappointment to him both then and later.

The two coronations were not prompted by the need to accommodate Henry within the governance of the realm, but by the military situation in France – a greater visibility as king and heightened legitimacy as a result of the ancient ceremonies would encourage Frenchmen to accept his claim – and nor did they result in Henry becoming directly involved in royal business between the tender ages of eight and ten. Nevertheless, from his return from France onwards, Henry was more publicly visible, and there was an understanding that it would not be that long before he took power into his own hands. In 1432 his tutor, the Earl of Warwick, reported him as being impatient with restrictions and having an awareness of his regality, but complained that Henry 'hath been stirred by some from his learning and spoken to of diverse matiers not behovefull', in other words that someone had been trying to involve Henry in (political) matters not suitable for his tender age.[3] This seems likely to have been prompted by the king's uncle, Humphrey, Duke of Gloucester, trying to use the king in his ongoing political struggle with Cardinal Beaufort, rather than genuine precociousness in Henry, and is also early evidence that Henry was easily influenced – unsurprising in the boy, but also prevalent in the adult. In 1434 the royal council praised his 'great understanding and feeling as ever they knew or saw in any prince, or other person of his age', but went on to say, reasonably enough, that he did not yet have sufficient knowledge or experience to dispense with the council, which administered government on the young king's behalf.[4] It was, in fact, the death of his elder uncle Bedford, regent of English

France, on 14 September 1435 that pushed the adolescent Henry into closer involvement in the active ruling of his kingdoms. He was present at a meeting of the royal council on 1 October 1435, the first evidence of the appearance of a personal act of government was on 10 April 1436, and in July and August Henry was personally signing writs. In May 1436 the Earl of Warwick resigned as his tutor, citing the need to focus on his own affairs, and Henry was free to rule. One further influence was removed soon afterwards: on 3 January 1437, after a period of illness, Henry's mother, Queen Catherine, died at the age of just thirty-five.

The young king was not just surrounded by adults. Some sons of members of the nobility were required to be resident in the royal household, in an attempt to strengthen the links between the future adult and his leading lords, and Henry formed close attachments to more than one. Perhaps the most important was Gilles, a younger son of the Duke of Brittany, who had been sent to the English court in 1432; they became firm friends and Gilles offered his service to Henry, proving loyal despite his father's defection to the King of France. Henry Beauchamp, four years younger than Henry and the son of Henry's tutor, the Earl of Warwick, also became close to the king, who showered him with marks of favour until Beauchamp's early death, aged twenty-one, in 1446.

Henry received the type of education typical of the royal family and the nobility at this time, balancing book-learning with chivalric attainments both social – courtesy and good behaviour – and physical, including military exercises. The adult Henry was fluent in French as well as English, and was able to read in Latin. He also seems to have had an interest in old texts and chronicles, evidenced in the crisis of 1460 when Richard, Duke of York claimed the throne and parliament asked the king to counter his claim from his own knowledge of 'many diverse writings and chronicles'.[5] There were also a string of works addressed or dedicated to him which proffered advice on being a king. Some of these comprised direct models for Henry to emulate, such as a life of his father,[6] and a *Life of Saint Edmund*, which depicted the Anglo-Saxon royal saint as a perfect blend of piety and chivalry.[7] Some contained more generic advice, such as the *Tractatus de Regimine Principium ad Regem Henricum Sextum* (*On the Rule of Princes to Henry VI*), almost certainly presented to Henry in the later 1430s or early 1440s, which placed an unusually strong emphasis on Christian kingship.[8] This flood of advice literature could, perhaps, indicate some anxiety about Henry's emerging personality among Henry's circle and family, who were responsible for the commissioning or authorship of some of these works. There is, though, no evidence that Henry either read any of them – or, if he did, that he took any of the advice on board.

There survives an unusual snapshot of Henry as a boy of twelve, when, in the midst of a dire financial crisis provoked by the ongoing war in France, the entire royal household decamped to the Suffolk monastery of Bury St Edmunds for four months, thereby passing on the bill for their upkeep from the royal Exchequer to the monastery's abbot. Two aspects stand out from the brief account of the visit that the abbot copied into his register. Henry, perhaps a little surprisingly in light of Blacman's picture of him as a man more given to prayer than 'practising vain sports and pursuits',[9] regularly hunted, both with dogs and hawks, and fished. While such pursuits were perhaps the quintessential leisure activity of the upper classes, there is little other evidence of Henry enjoying physical activities as anything other than occasional pastimes. The other striking aspect of the description of Henry's stay at Bury was the notable piety he displayed: in the welcoming ceremony, he knelt to worship the image of the cross in the monastery precinct and then kissed it when it was brought to him; at the end of his stay he demanded to be admitted to the fraternity of the monastery, as did a number of his nobles who had stayed with him there. The abbot's description of this contains a note of surprise, as Henry was the patron and representative of the founder of the abbey, so to be part of the fraternity was rather superfluous; but it was Henry's pious desire, superfluous or not, so the abbot acceded.[10]

If there was one thing missing from an upbringing that was designed to prepare Henry to be an active king, it was, in the words of one of his most significant biographers, 'the creation of an environment in which he could develop sound, independent judgement that would eventually free him from the tutelage of his uncles and councillors'.[11] His adolescent years were dominated by the forceful personalities of his uncles, Gloucester and Bedford, and his great-uncle, Cardinal Henry Beaufort, while as an adult he seems to have relied to an excessive and dangerous degree on a number of powerful personalities, most particularly his successive leading ministers, the Dukes of Suffolk and

Somerset, and his wife, Margaret of Anjou. Yet such an outcome was not inevitable: Richard II, who came to the throne at the age of ten in 1377, had also grown up alongside powerful, manipulative uncles, John of Gaunt and Thomas of Woodstock, and yet from very early on had tried to assert his independence from them – admittedly with disastrous results. Had Henry VI had a more forceful personality, he might have been able to play the dominating role in government and war that the role of king demanded. Instead his energies seem to have been devoted less to governance and politics than to something rather more personal: his soul.

The most important facet of Henry's emerging royal personality was his piety. Like all medieval monarchs, he had been instructed in the Christian faith from an early age. His first confessor was in office by 1424 (when he was three), and there were a number of chaplains and confessors around him from then onwards. Henry visited, and resided in, monasteries more often than was normal for kings in this period, and his interest in Anglo-Saxon saint-kings such as Edmund, Fremund and Alfred was stimulated during these visits and by manuscripts made to commemorate them (for an example, see plate 2).

Put kindly, Henry had a deep, sincere and prominent faith; put unkindly, his was an excessive, consuming and compulsive religiosity. Deep piety was not in itself a barrier to effective kingship. Indeed, the advice literature to kings commended personal devotion, while contemporaries expected public acts of alms-giving and religious ceremonial, and English kings swore to uphold the peace of the Church in their coronation oaths. When combined with other qualities, piety could enhance effective kingship, and Henry would have been very much aware of his direct ancestor, Louis IX of France, who became St Louis, canonized twenty-seven years after his death in 1270. Often considered the epitome of Christian kingship, Louis had been an effective ruler of France in many respects, as a law-giver, administrator and in mobilizing the resources of his kingdom into two mighty crusades, although both were disastrous failures. Louis's sanctity reinforced his authority: one contemporary stated that 'he exercised priesthood like a king and kingship like a priest'.[12]

That was not the case for Henry. Two accounts, one written by a foreign observer at close quarters to the sixteen-year-old monarch and the other by one who knew him in his mature years, show this clearly. The later medieval papacy placed emphasis on an individual's exemplary life rather than on the violent death, the 'martyrdom', that governed the sanctity of so many earlier saints, and it is a description of such an exemplary life that fills the account by John Blacman, his former chaplain. While the purpose of Blacman's text was clearly to provide a description of Henry's saintliness during his lifetime, rather than an account of his reign, he knew Henry well and was an eyewitness to some of the events he describes, and clearly spoke to others who served Henry at different periods of his life. Treated with caution, and placed within the context of other evidence, Blacman's depiction of Henry has some strength.

The picture of Henry given by Blacman is of a virtuous

man, with a fear of God, who was a diligent worshipper, 'more given to God and to devout prayer than to handling worldly and temporal things'. He was humble in his devotions, 'so that even when decked with the kingly ornaments and crowned with the royal diadem he made it a duty to bow before the lord as deep in prayer as any young monk might have done'. Henry was chaste, eschewing all licentiousness in word and deed while he was young until his marriage to Margaret, to whom 'he kept his marriage vow wholly and sincerely'. He could not abide even seeing nakedness, lest he be 'snared by unlawful desire', and fled from the sight of unclothed bathers at Bath.[13] He was not avaricious but generous to his servants and to the Church. Henry was also humble in his dress, and wished nothing better than to pray or read rather than attend to business; he was, in particular, patient in the face of many adversities and compassionate and merciful towards those who wronged him.

Fifty years earlier than the composition of Blacman's account, a papal tax collector, Piero da Monte, was intermittently at Henry's court and met the king on a number of occasions. In 1437, in a letter to the Archbishop of Florence, he wrote a description of the young king. Although still of tender years, commented da Monte, Henry had an old man's sense, prudence and gravity. Each day he read the divine office with a priest, attended Mass and most devoutly observed fasts, and restrained his body through abstinence and continence, in particular through fleeing the sight and speech of women. Those who knew him well affirmed that he was a virgin, and had resolved not to have intercourse with any woman unless within the bonds of marriage. He detested scurrilous games, obscene words and indecent mimes and plays. Amidst ceremony and crowds he showed humility, among attendants and body-guards an easy accessibility, amidst banquets abstinence. His singular reverence for, and devotion to, the Church and the pope were to be marvelled at in one so young. He seemed, concluded da Monte, 'not a king or a secular prince ... but a monk or a religious man, more religious than a man of religion'.[14]

The striking similarities of the two descriptions by two very different individuals half a century apart can in part be explained by the fact that these qualities – which contemporary advice literature found desirable – were not singular to Henry but were generic to descriptions of princes. The civil servant and versifier Thomas Hoccleve's *Regement of Princes*, composed some decades before for Henry VI's father when Prince of Wales, urged him among other things to patience (the gentle sufferance of wrongs), mercy and chastity – which was convenable and convenient for a king; and 'who so chaste shall live / Must scourge his fleshly lust with abstinence'.[15] Meanwhile, the *Tractatus de Regimine Principum*, a treatise of the duties of a king, written for and presented to Henry probably in the late 1430s, places much emphasis on a king's private devotions, urging that a king must try to live like Christ, but also on his patronage of learning and the universities, another prominent element of Henry's piety. Indeed, da Monte's language was particularly reminiscent of hagiography, idealized biographies of religious figures. Yet literary precedent is only half the story. Both da Monte and Blacman contain unique material. Moreover, their descriptions of the king, so similar despite being written fifty years apart by such different men, chime with Henry's actions throughout his lifetime, while other contemporary comments fit with this picture of a pious, meek and prudish king. For example Abbot Whetehamstede of St Albans, who met Henry on a number of occasions, described him (admittedly after his deposition in 1461) as a king who did not cultivate the art of war, but instead was a 'mild-spoken, pious king', adding critically that he was 'half-witted in affairs of state'.[16] John Rous, connected with Henry's Beaufort relatives, commented that 'To God and the Virgin Mary he was most devoted, but to the world and worldly things he was least devoted, always committing them to the Council.'[17] Henry also owned a vernacular bible, highly unusual at this date, and it can be presumed that such an unusual item was used by the owner. The bible still survives in the Bodleian Library in Oxford (plate 3). The confluence of all the evidence makes the picture compelling: so many sources paint this same image of a pious man, concerned with religious matters to the point of prejudicing his royal duties.

Henry's marriage presents another set of problems and conflicting evidence within this framework of a spiritual king. It was not until 1445, by which time Henry was twenty-three, that he was finally married, to Margaret, daughter of a great French nobleman, René, Duke of Anjou, in a ceremony away from the main centres of the English monarchy, at Titchfield Abbey in Hampshire on

22 April 1445, with the ceremony conducted by Henry's confessor, William Aiscough, Bishop of Salisbury. It was extraordinary that Henry's marriage took so long to be arranged, given both the ever-present threat of disease and death in war even for kings, and also the scarcity of male members of the Lancastrian dynasty who could succeed him. Most kings were married in their teens, in part so they could produce children more quickly, but on occasions when other kings had married late, such as Henry V and Edward IV, they had several brothers who could have succeeded them without question, thus providing dynastic security. Henry had only his uncle, Duke Humphrey, who was childless and, with his wife imprisoned for life for treason from 1441, was unlikely to produce children. Other male relatives were not in a position to succeed. The Beaufort family, descended from an illegitimate liaison of Henry's great-grandfather, John of Gaunt, had been formally disbarred from succeeding to the throne, while Henry's two half-brothers, Edmund and Jasper Tudor, had no drop of English royal blood in their veins, being the issue of Queen Catherine's second marriage to Owen Tudor. Thus Henry, and England, needed a son and heir.

Even after the marriage took place, it was to be eight years before Margaret produced her one child, Edward. The dynastic situation had become even more acute after Gloucester's death in 1447, as Henry was the only male of the house of Lancaster left alive, and England only a single accident or fatal illness away from dynastic chaos. Such a delay between marriage and progeny was not unprecedented, but in Henry and Margaret's case people started speculating about the reason for the delay. On 11 January 1447 John Page of London, a draper, was indicted for alleging that when Henry wished 'to have his sport' with his queen, his confessor Bishop Aiscough prevented him from coming 'nigh her'.[18] This may have reflected the unpopularity of Aiscough and others at the court rather than the reality, but the perception of Henry as being ruled by his spiritual advisers was not unique to this incautious London merchant, and fits with the picture given by da Monte and Blacman. Predictably enough, however, in the male-oriented world of the fifteenth century Margaret also took the blame for the couple's lack of children: one man from Canterbury was alleged to have said that 'our queen was none able to be Queen of England . . . for because she beareth no child, and because that we have no prince in this land.'[19] In the more polarized and factionalized world of the later 1450s and early 1460s it was alleged that Prince Edward was not Henry's son but a product of Margaret's adultery. While easy to explain as a slur by Margaret's and Henry's political enemies, it may have been effective as propaganda, drawing as it did on earlier rumours and innuendos about the royal couple.

Henry's attitude towards his marriage is more difficult to gauge. Da Monte, writing of the teenage Henry, was told that he had resolved not to have intercourse with any woman unless within the bonds of marriage. Blacman, fifty years later, described Henry as keeping 'his marriage vow wholly and sincerely, even in the absences of lady [Margaret], which were sometimes very long: never dealing unchastely with any other woman. Neither when they lived together did he use his wife unseemly, but with all honesty and gravity.'[20] Sex within marriage, condoned and encouraged by the Church, should not, therefore, have been a moral problem for Henry. Yet one might wonder if there were more psychological issues. Henry, as portrayed by Blacman, avoided the sight of the female body, apparently averting his eyes and leaving the room when confronted by 'a show of young ladies with bared bosoms who were to dance in that guise before the king, perhaps to prove him, or to entice his youthful mind'.[21] Da Monte noted that 'The sight and conversation of women he avoided, quoting from the gospel: "he who casts his eyes on a woman so as to lust after her has already committed adultery with her in his heart".'[22] Both comments might of course be read in other ways – chastity was essentially for the saintly picture Blacman was painting; da Monte's comments were approving of Henry's attitude, showing a young man able to resist temptation – but much of the evidence that historians have used to argue for normality in Henry's attitude towards marriage generally, and his marriage with Margaret in particular, is ambivalent.

During the long-drawn-out search for a bride for Henry, before Margaret of Anjou was settled on, there was some consideration of the daughters of the Count of Armagnac, in the south-west of France. Ambassadors were despatched in 1442 with instructions, written by the king's secretary, Thomas Bekynton, which included an order that portraits be made of the girls 'in their kirtles simple, and their faces, like as you see their stature and their beauty and colour of skin and their countenances, with all manner of features'.

The portraits were to be delivered in all haste 'to the king, and he to appoint and sign which he likes'.[23] Clearly this could reflect the king's actual instructions, revealing a healthy interest in the looks of potential brides; yet the phrasing suggests this is at one remove, as if Bekynton or others were trying to engage Henry's enthusiasm and interest in the matter, rather than the king being eager. A story, recounted second-hand to the Duchess of Milan ten years later, recorded that Henry was so eager to see Margaret after she had disembarked that he dressed as a squire to deliver her a letter, and Margaret, unknowing, kept him on his knees while she read the letter and he took stock of her. This tale almost certainly has its basis in chivalric romance rather than fact.[24] Another description, used as evidence of Henry and Margaret's happy marriage, also needs revision. An aside in a court manual reported Henry and Margaret receiving New Year's gifts together in bed in the king's chamber, suggesting a picture of uxorious comfort and familiarity. The text, though, states 'beddes' rather than 'bed', and although it does use the singular of 'chamber', by the following reign, however, the same source makes it absolutely clear that Edward IV and Elizabeth Woodville were receiving their gifts in bed in separate chambers.[25]

Inextricably linked with Henry's piety are his building projects. Eton College (founded in 1440) and King's College, Cambridge (1441) have been the focus of much attention, therefore, as almost the only positive achievements of Henry's reign, not least because they exist today in much the same form as when they were established.

Both were indisputably royal foundations, but nonetheless there has been some question over Henry's personal contribution to the establishment of Eton and King's. While all was done in the king's name, others have been credited with being the real inspiration and guiding lights behind the foundations, pushing Henry into more ambitious designs. Candidates include Henry's clever secretary Thomas Bekynton and the influential William Waynflete, Bishop of Winchester, both of whom had been educated at institutions with the same links between school and college as that proposed between Eton and King's. It is also clear that the Duke of Suffolk, the king's leading minister in the 1440s, made many of the day-to-day decisions and played a major role in the early years of both colleges. A considerable body of contemporary opinion sought to use English lands granted to religious houses which were under the direct control of foreign (French) monasteries, and which had been seized at the resumption of the Hundred Years War in 1415, for religious foundations. Given that much of Eton's endowment was from these lands, one historian has argued that 'The vision was less Henry's and rather the result of a pre-existing pressure.'[26]

If Henry was less directly involved, then the purpose of the colleges fits neatly within a tradition of religious foundations designed to bolster and project the image of the English monarchy and the Lancastrian dynasty and to elevate the crown far above its greatest subjects, thus giving the foundations a political rather than a religious purpose. Certainly it is true that most of Henry VI's predecessors and successors had made major initiatives towards the establishment of religious foundations or the enhancement of existing institutions. Yet placing the foundations within this existing tradition has the effect of rather minimizing what was achieved: unlike his predecessors or successors, Henry established educational institutions rather than just houses of prayer or elaborate venues for a monarch's burial (although Henry may have seen Eton as his preferred place of interment).

The evidence, however, suggests very strongly that Henry was the instigator or, even if the idea was suggested to him by others, that he enthusiastically embraced it. Given Henry's piety in general and his adulation of King Alfred, an educational reformer, in particular, such institutions would have fitted perfectly with how Henry saw his role. Indeed, he tried to have Alfred canonized as a saint in 1442; the sudden flowering of interest in the canonization at exactly the time that Henry was setting up his educational institutions, as well as the fact that one of Henry's closest advisers, Adam Moleyns, was sent to Rome to argue the case to the pope, strongly suggest that it was Henry's personal initiative. Beyond his own foundations Henry was a generous educational patron, giving a large donation of books from the royal library to the newly established All Souls College at Oxford in 1440, and in 1445 he endowed a new library at Salisbury Cathedral. In response to a petition by King's College, Cambridge, Henry granted £20 due to him from the forfeited goods of a felon, adding, however, it was 'to be employed upon books and other necessary stuff'.[27]

More importantly, Henry took a close personal interest

in his collegiate foundations that has no parallel in his attitude towards other public business. Several documents are explicit about Henry's engagement in the foundations, but the most extraordinary was written in 1448. It is headed 'My [Henry's] will and my intent', and in it the king stated that:

for as much as it hath liked unto our lord for to suffer and grant me grace for the premier notable work purposed by me after I, by his blessed sufferance, took unto myself the rule of my said Realms, for to erect, found and establish unto the honour and worship of his name specially and of the blessed virgin our lady saint Mary, [to] increase of virtues, and cunning in [the] expansion and [the] establishment of Christian faith, my two Colleges Royal, one called the College royal of our lady of Eton beside Windsor, and the other called the College royal of our lady and saint Nicholas of Cambridge.[28]

The document then sets out the exact dimensions of all the buildings, including the main choir of the church at Eton, which was to be 207 feet long, 32 broad and 80 high – an extraordinary size, surpassed only by the projected length of King's, which was to be 288 feet. A later design extended the length of Eton's church to 318 feet. Phrased throughout in the first person (rather than the normal royal 'we'), and surely reflecting Henry's personal vision for his foundations, the document was sealed and 'signed with my own hand'.[29] It is impossible to dismiss this unusual and personal statement, shorn of the normal excessive verbiage and well-worn phrases of the royal chancery, as anything other than Henry's direct wishes. In addition, a considerable number of other documents relating to both colleges were initialled 'RH' – 'Rex Henricus' – in his own hand and show that he took a direct interest in the building, down to the smallest details. There is yet more evidence of Henry's personal involvement with the projects. He laid the foundation stones at both institutions. Favouring residence at Windsor so he could supervise the building works at Eton, he also visited Cambridge on at least ten occasions between 1441 and 1461, trips that were usually connected with the college he was building. He also sought to secure papal bulls for an extraordinary set of ecclesiastical privileges to ensure that Eton and King's College stood apart from and far above other educational institutions. Henry's almost childlike personality perhaps emerges most clearly in his devotion to these two cherished building projects. Such was his enthusiasm to see progress on them that in February 1443 his secretary, Thomas Bekynton, wrote to Vincent Clement, Henry's chief agent in Rome, urging Clement to push the king's requests to the pope for spiritual privileges for Eton and King's. The king, wrote Bekynton, was pestering him daily, asking: 'When will we have news from Master Vincent?'[30]

Henry devoted huge financial resources to the projects, endowing them with land (not just from confiscated foreign priories but also with other estates), and providing both with building funds running at approximately £1,000 each annually. During the period 1444–61, when the French war and then civil faction reduced the crown to almost total poverty, spending an estimated £15,000–£16,000 on each foundation was a great commitment, and indeed provoked parliament to complain in 1450 that the two colleges were 'prejudicial to your highness and very burdensome and harmful to your liege people of this your realm'.[31]

Burdensome or not, the two colleges were almost the only tangible achievements of Henry's reign. Seven years of building at Eton were abandoned in 1448 in order to start again on even more grandiose designs, and continued sporadically during the 1450s. Eton was briefly threatened by the Yorkist takeover after 1461 but Edward IV was eventually to relent and allow its continuation, though on a more moderate scale. King's also continued to be built during the 1450s, but the sheer scale of the chapel in particular meant that it was not completed until Henry VIII's reign. Nonetheless, both had scholars during the 1450s, and both became highly prestigious educational institutions, and remain so to this day.

While piety may have been Henry's defining characteristic, it did not and could not impinge on certain aspects of being a late-medieval king. One of those was the need to appear kingly, to dress in a magnificent way, and for his court to overawe his subjects and foreign visitors alike. The advice manuals were all in agreement on this point, and even the arch-pragmatist, Sir John Fortescue, concerned with restraining the spending power of late-medieval kings, acknowledged the point that: 'it shall need that the king have such treasure, as he may make new buildings when he will, for his pleasure and magnificence; and as he may buy him riche clothes, riche furs . . . and other jewels and ornaments convenient to his estate royal.' This was so, Fortescue added, as 'For if a king did not so, nor might do, he lived then not like his estate, but rather in misery, and in more subjection that doth a private person.'[32]

Blacman, seeking to portray Henry's humility, got rather carried away in his depiction of a dowdy king, asserting that, among other things, 'it is well known that from his youth up', Henry 'always wore round-toed shoes and boots like a farmer's . . . [and] customarily wore a long gown with a rolled hood like a townsman . . . rejecting expressly all curious fashion of clothing', while at the principal feasts of the year, particularly those few days in the year on which it was customary for English kings to wear their crown, he would wear a hair shirt so that 'all pride and vain glory, such as is apt to be engendered by pomp, might be repressed'.[33]

Henry, though, did not 'always' wear humble clothes; in fact, there is evidence of considerable luxury. In 1438–9, in his late teens, his wardrobe accounts reveal a number of high-quality items made for him: a short gown of black velvet, furred with the skins of at least 220 martens; another velvet gown adorned with gold, pearls and furred with sable; six other gowns of scarlet, red and russet, furred with martens; a hunting gown of green cloth; a scarlet mantle and two black riding hoods; dozens of pairs of black hose; handkerchiefs and other accoutrements.[34] Such a level of expenditure, moreover, was the norm in years to come. In 1443–4 the quality and quantity of items of clothing made for the king was similar. These included:

a gown of black velvet, furred with the skins of 234 martens; a black velvet hat, furred with ermine; a velvet tabard, furred with ermine; a kirtle of velvet; a long gown of purple velvet, furred with martens; another long gown of velvet, adorned with cloth of gold; a long cloth gown lined with ermine; a scarlet gown; a purple gown; and a red-velvet mantle for the feast of St George, embroidered with the arms of the saint.[35] Nor was such expenditure in vain. French ambassadors meeting Henry at Westminster in 1445 were impressed by his appearance, noting in particular his clothing, a 'rich robe down to the ground, of red cloth of gold', and his surroundings, as he was seated beneath tapestries 'of gold, very rich'.[36]

Henry's court is often thought of as 'shabby and indigent', especially in comparison with the splendour of those dynasties to come.[37] Although this may have been the case in the years following Henry's collapse in 1453, it was demonstrably not true earlier in his reign. In the eyes of foreign observers, the Lancastrian court dazzled and was extravagant enough to generate complaint in the eyes of the taxpayers. Henry's royal chapel, comprising a dean, thirty singers, two priests, one choirmaster, one master of grammar, one serjeant, one yeoman, ten choirboys and two servants, so impressed a visiting Portuguese nobleman that he asked the then dean, William Say, to write its procedures and ordinances down so he could present them to his own monarch; the manuscript, probably based on a set of English ordinances now lost, still survives in a Portuguese archive.[38] David Starkey has proved that part of an influential text on the ceremonial, procedure and organization of the royal household, known as the *Ryalle Book*, previously thought to be from the reign of Henry VII, in fact dates in part from that of Henry VI.[39] It describes in minute detail the great days of state when the king wore his crown, led a procession to the chapel where he attended a special Mass, had a formal dinner with a multitude of guests in his hall or chamber, then mingled with them rather more informally over dessert and wine, part of the occasion known as the 'void'. Henry, contrary to a common perception of him, lived at the centre of a magnificent court, at times perhaps comprising 1,200 people, whose ceremonial impressed those who came into contact with it. He was also, at first glance at least, physically impressive. When his tomb was opened in 1910 his bones were examined, and it was discovered that Henry was at least five feet nine inches in height, perhaps a little taller, well above average height for the time. The man at the heart of this court looked and dressed like a king. Whether he acted as a king should is another matter.

Henry had to engage with a further requirement of kingship, that of government, and it was here that, right from the outset of his majority, he fell noticeably short of what was necessary. Late-medieval kings were expected to govern personally. While they had a more or less formalized council that had authority to take some decisions, offer advice on many subjects, and was certainly expected to carry out executive work, the king himself was required to make big decisions – to summon a parliament, go to war and make peace, appoint councillors and his chief officers – while being seen to take advice from his officials and from both lay and spiritual peers, and to attend himself to matters of grace. The latter were decisions reserved to the king alone and included grants of pardon for crimes, of annuities, of lands, of wardship, of offices on the king's estates, and of presentation to Church livings, among many other things.

Kings received thousands of petitions a year in writing and in person, and had a duty to consider them, weigh them, grant some but not all and to keep the interests of the crown in mind. Henry, seemingly, considered none of these things. Instead he appeared to grant almost everything. Petitions that were refused are hard to find for any king, but there is almost no evidence that Henry turned any down. It is in any case clear that Henry granted so many that there were very serious repercussions for his subjects and his government; by 1450, his generosity threatened his tenure of the crown.

Carelessness, lack of attention to detail and sheer incompetence were the hallmarks of the king's involvement in government. In February 1438 the same landed estate was granted to two different individuals on consecutive days. Two months later, a grant to Walter Strickland of an office in the king's lordship of Kendal was qualified so that it could only be made 'provided that the office shall not have been granted previously to any other person'.[40] Such qualifying clauses were not usually to be found under other kings, who would have delayed making any grant until a clerk could check whether or not it was still in the king's gift. Those around Henry who had his and the kingdom's best interests at heart were well aware of the problem and tried to open his eyes to the issues. As early as February 1438, the clerk of the royal council, Henry Benet, noted that he had to speak to the king 'to be aware how that he granted pardons or else how that he does them to be amended for he does to himself therein great damage, and now late in a pardon that he granted unto a customs official the which lost the King 2,000 marks'[41] (a mark was two-thirds of a pound). The following day Benet wrote a further note that he should speak to the king about the loss of 1,000 marks which he had sustained by the grant made of the constable-ship of the castle of Chirk.

In 1444 ordinances were drawn up by the council to address the issue of the king's endless bounty to all who asked it of him. While respecting the king's power to do as he wished, they advised that all petitions be scrutinized by a number of assessors: if they were matters of justice they would go to the council; if matters of grace they would go to Henry. But in the latter case a clear summary of the contents would be written on the back of the petition to help the king assess it, and decide whether he ought to refer it to the council for advice. The ordinances also speci-fied the standard and very bureaucratic process by which such petitions should then be executed, which many grants made by Henry had been bypassing; the ordinances expli-citly stated that the more hands a grant passed through, the more likely it was that any hurt to the king or prejudice to other persons would be noticed and eschewed. To many kings, any such attempt to restrict their decision-making would have been a direct assault on the royal prerogative and an insult to their competence, but Henry approved it without a murmur. Regrettably for his government, the ordinances had only a limited impact, both in terms of numbers of petitions they affected and the duration for which they, in practice, lasted, as Henry was soon carelessly signing petitions drawn up by the petitioners in a manner specifically designed to avoid oversight, limit the bureaucratic process and to expedite the benefits to the grantee.

Matters of grace had to be carried out by the king, rather than any other agency, and Henry, in his unique way, did carry them out. There were many, and we know that Henry did indeed look at most of them, as he signed a great number – 1,407 alone among the warrants for the Great Seal (the final administrative stage before the formal grant was issued to the recipient) between 1437 and 1453. Given this, and with patronage very much part of the exercise of government, we can hardly dismiss Henry as 'playing no operational part in government for years'.[42] Yet so many of Henry's interventions in government bear the hallmark not of his rather limited interest in justice, warfare or statesmanship, but of his piety. In a famous case of July 1444, one Thomas Kerver was accused on six counts of treason, and found guilty in five. Not content with this – probably because the one 'not guilty' verdict was that of the key crime of inciting others to kill the king – members of the council and the royal household organized a second trial, in order to find Kerver guilty of all six counts, and thus to use him as an example to discourage any others from such treasonous thoughts and actions. But, condemned to a traitor's death by hanging, drawing and quartering, Kerver was then pardoned at the last minute by

Henry on the grounds that the feast of the Assumption – which had special importance for his royal foundation at Eton College – was imminent. Given that this pardon went directly against the wishes of those around Henry, it is good evidence not only of his capacity to make his own decisions, but also of the basis on which he made them: this decision reflected his spiritual priorities, not the political ones of his advisers.

Kerver's case is not the only example of such pious reasons behind Henry's decisions. Pardons were issued to members of the Duke of Gloucester's household in 1447 on exactly the same grounds of the forthcoming feast of the Assumption. In November the same year, Henry granted a charter to the priory of Bridlington, which he signed 'RH', adding a Latin note in his own handwriting (see plate 9) to the effect that the grant was his alms to St John of Bridlington, a saint whose cult had close associations with the Lancastrian dynasty. Other examples of Henry's occasional personal pious interventions are written on the petitions handed to the king by the chamberlain or clerk in the royal presence, but there is no reason to doubt they reflect Henry's personal words or opinions. In 1448, for example, the king, 'of his own mere motion without stirring or moving by any person earthly for the devotion that he hath to the blessed Virgin our lady Saint Mary', granted a petition by the priory of Our Lady of Walsingham, and returned it with his own hands to the prior;[43] a year earlier, a petition by a house of friars at Marlborough to have fees liable in the chancery waived was granted by the king, 'considering the great poverty of the house'.[44] Very occasional additions also written by the chamberlain on petitions as if by the king directly, reflecting technical or legal additions, qualifications or changes, may also reflect Henry's thoughts, but might also suggest the expertise or advice of councillors, household men or administrators present. The pious statements of intent are less plausibly those of others.

In areas of government other than matters of grace, Henry played a less obvious role than other medieval kings. He seemingly had little interest in the process of government, wished to avoid problems, and was quite content for others to do as much as they could, so he could concentrate on other projects and interests that were more important to him. Henry's lack of interest in government and politics is neatly encapsulated by Blacman's anecdote of how one night, when Henry was sitting with his chaplain, a 'mighty duke of the realm' knocked at the door and the king complained: 'they do so interrupt me that by day or night I can hardly snatch a moment to be refreshed by reading of any holy teaching without disturbance'.[45] While the incident itself is hardly verifiable, and clearly fulfils Blacman's brief of portraying Henry in a saintly way, it does, in the context of the records, have the ring of authenticity. Man-management of such great lords, whose cares were those of both Henry's state and their own localities, was critical to good kingship. It is clear that as the political heavyweights of Henry's minority, Gloucester and Beaufort, began to fade from the political scene after 1440, Henry did not emerge as the centre of all operations. Instead, he left an unusual amount of business to others. The royal council, according to one influential view, played an unusually prominent role under the adult Henry until about 1445; and from then until 1450, a group led by the Duke of Suffolk and comprising Lord Say, Adam Moleyns, William Aiscough and others seems to have dominated government.[46] The extent to which Henry made decisions is debatable, but it was nonetheless obvious to at least some contemporaries that he was not ruling as he should.

Differing theories have been put forward for Henry's lack of engagement with the normal processes of government. One proposes that Henry was simply not up to the job of ruling, and the absence of his royal will forced others to try to rule in his name. Others have suggested that Henry, as he grew up, became rather dependent on others ruling in his stead, though still capable of making judgements. Much of the available evidence, indeed, would suggest that while Henry did make decisions, he only did so on an occasional basis on subjects of particular interest to him; in this way, he was usually content to sign whatever was put in front of him without much thought to the consequences, letting others do most of the work.

This 'occasional' king is consequently one in whose reign much care must be taken when assessing the decision-making process. Crucially, however, those areas where we can see Henry's active involvement – both bigger policy decisions, such as the foundation of Eton and King's and the diplomacy that sought peace with France throughout most of the 1440s, and occasional interventions in minor matters – are frequently those that accord with Henry's religiosity, from pardons in honour of a forthcoming saint's day to the foundation of religious institutions 'according to the measure of our devotion'. We should see Henry's piety as the keynote of his kingship. One does not need to accept uncritically Blacman's description, or to believe Henry a non-canonized saint, to see that as a man or as a king his priorities were more spiritual than temporal, devotional rather than martial, and, while admirable in their own way, were not what was required of a fifteenth-century king – most particularly one who had inherited, alongside the undisputed crown of England, the disputed crown of a war-torn France.

It is on the absence of any martial activity during the later 1430s and 1440s that the most damning indictment of Henry's kingship can be built. Parliament implied during Henry's minority that a king had the personal duty of attendance to the actual defence of the land.[47] The advice manuals were unanimous that, while peace was desirable, war should be prosecuted in the defence of a king's rights and his kingdom, and that the king himself should lead and fight in war. Frulovisi's life of Henry V contained a direct address to Henry VI, in which he was enjoined that 'thou shalt seek peace and rest with victory to both thy realms by thy virtue and battle, and by those feats by which thy Father tamed both his adversaries and thine'.[48] While it is not known if Henry ever read these works, or other advice literature (and one should not build too much on these as direct influences on him), it is clear that the expectation that Henry should lead an army to France was both widespread and disappointed. Henry was the only king of medieval England (other than the boy-king Edward V) who did not lead an army in war against a foreign enemy, and in the circumstances of the 1440s this complete neglect of his personal duty was detrimental to his subjects and problematic for his kingship. Certainly, some contemporaries were caught complaining about it – Thomas Kerver, pardoned by Henry for treason, was alleged to have compared Henry unfavourably to the French Dauphin, Charles, who was said to have acted manfully in conquering English lands, and that Henry would have held those lands peacefully and quietly if he were of 'like stuff'.[49] In a letter of 1443 issued under his most personal seal, the signet, Henry wrote to William Wells, Bishop of Rochester. Noting the great army that the French were readying to attack Normandy and Gascony by land and sea, Henry describes how, by the advice of his council, a great army was being raised to resist them:

> nevertheless for as much as we know and consider well that the prosperity and welfare of princes and of their Realms, lands and subjects, and the getting and achieving of victories upon their enemies rests not principally in man's wisdom or strength nor in multitude of people, but in the hands, disposition and grace of God, the which it likes him to grant to those that set their hope and their trust principally in him and lowly sue and seek unto him . . . by sacrifice of humble and devout prayers, by fasting and by chastising of themselves by alms, deeds and other blessed works[50]

Henry therefore specified, at some length, how the bishop and his flock should pray for the success of his forces and the defence of all his realms. Similar letters were sent to other bishops. These epistles and the faith behind them are in many ways conventional, and appeals to God were part and parcel of any great military effort, but it remains striking that, in an hour of need, Henry's recourse was not to his martial duty but to his faith; it was not to lead troops in defence of his subjects but to organize prayer for them; it was not to his captains but to his bishops that he turned. Even when concerned with very earthly matters, Henry's eyes remained fixed on heaven.

The extent to which Henry's failure to go to war was a personal choice, reflecting a distaste of warfare and his Christian piety, or whether those around him, shuddering to think of the issues a malleable, inexperienced commander like Henry would have created as head of an army on foreign soil, discouraged him is not possible to establish, but perhaps his failure to lead his armies might have stemmed from both. Henry was also not clearly a natural warrior. Unlike his father, wounded at the Battle of Shrewsbury in 1403 at the age of sixteen and the victor of Agincourt at twenty-eight, or his supplanter, Edward IV, who fought in the front line at several battles, there is no evidence that Henry ever actually engaged in combat or 'wielded anything more lethal than a prayer-book'.[51]

When he reached the age of twenty-one in 1442, Henry had many of the attributes necessary in a king. He looked the part, tall and well attired, while his court impressed foreigners and subjects alike. He had a deep Christian piety that was expected of medieval kings, and had just embarked on two major building projects that reflected both this piety and the power of the Lancastrian monarchy. While he was not as active in government or as careful of the royal finances as might have been expected, these were not necessarily crippling faults in a king. Yet as the decade wore on the fault lines in Henry's kingship grew deeper rather than better: in particular his reliance on a chosen few to run his realm and his own failure to lead his desperate subjects in war. By 1450, both of Henry's realms, England and France, were in chaos, and criticism of his ministers and their policies, for which Henry was ultimately responsible, had reached fever pitch. By 1453 the French realm had been lost, and Henry had suffered an unprecedented mental and physical collapse brought on by the strain of domestic chaos and foreign defeat.

2
Policy and Profligacy, 1436–1453

By the time Henry came of age as king in 1436 his French realm faced significant challenges. England's possessions in France comprised Gascony in the south-west, held by the kings of England since 1154; the small but strategically vital town of Calais, taken by Edward III in 1347; and Normandy and parts of Maine, conquered by Henry V and other commanders between 1417 and 1429. During Henry VI's infancy, his uncle, John, Duke of Bedford, had continued the expansion of English territory as a result of important victories at the Battles of Cravant in 1423 and Verneuil in 1424 and England's alliance with the Duke of Burgundy, ruler of a wealthy, powerful state comprising the duchy of Burgundy in eastern France, but more importantly most of the Low Countries and parts of north-eastern France. The English advance had been checked with defeat at the siege of Orléans in 1429, however, and the French, inspired by Joan of Arc, had begun to retake English-held territory, though on a small scale. Joan was captured in 1430 and executed the following year, but this success was more than offset by the Duke of Burgundy's defection from the English alliance five years later. This defection had an immediate impact in the loss of Paris, seat of the English administration, a blow compounded a few weeks later by the death of the able Duke of Bedford. The fourteen-year-old Henry felt the sting of betrayal keenly; he burst into tears on receipt of a letter from Burgundy that omitted to address him as Burgundy's sovereign lord. In a characteristically pious and generous gesture, Henry sent the purported head of St Anne to Cardinal Albergati, who had led the papal delegation at the Congress of Arras, where Burgundy had announced his betrayal – though it is less clear that the cardinal deserved Henry's gratitude: the papal delegation in part facilitated the Franco-Burgundian reconciliation.

The teenage Henry VI and his council faced a major dilemma. English conquest of the rest of France was now almost unachievable, but the defence of Normandy, Gascony and Calais remained a realistic goal – the key question was how. Continue to prosecute a defensive war for as long as it took, or seek a long-term peace with the French? France, though, was unlikely to accept easily the permanent loss of Normandy, nor would the English cede Henry's claim to the French throne. On the other hand, neither side could continue to fight indefinitely. Both sides were war-weary and financially exhausted, although the English Exchequer was in a worse state than the French treasury. There also remained a vocal party in England, led by Henry V's brother, Humphrey, Duke of Gloucester, who, clinging to Henry V's legacy, opposed any concessions to the French.

In general, though not consistently, peace was the course chosen by Henry VI and his government over the next decade. As always with Henry VI, there is some debate over the extent to which he himself was the author and architect of the policy or whether he was simply under the thumb of key advisers, most particularly the ageing Cardinal Beaufort (who died in 1447) and William, Duke of Suffolk, both of whom certainly advocated a peace policy in these years as the most practical solution to the problem of the French war. A pacifist approach was evidently something that would fit with Henry's wishes, both in practical terms but also with his beliefs. Henry was not a warrior king; he never led an army to France as an adult, and it was only briefly considered once as a possibility when he was fourteen, in the crisis of 1436 when the Duke of Burgundy threatened English-held Calais. A letter in his name on 16 June that year stated that 'for the tuition and defence of the said town we dispose us with God's mercy to give recourse there to in our person as to the town in the World most needful for this our Realm'. By the end of June another letter noted that he was instead going to Canterbury to oversee the departure of the army, and it was Humphrey, Duke of Gloucester, who chased the Duke of Burgundy away.[1] The dominant aspect of his personality, his piety, would have seen the effusion of Christian blood as something to avoid, something explicitly stated in several letters and declarations by Henry during the increasingly crisis-ridden 1440s. Such devout statements were commonplace in diplomatic correspondence in the period, but Henry's are perhaps more fulsome than most, and fit with what we can see of his character. Significantly, too, there is better evidence for Henry's personal engagement in the process of peacemaking than in other areas of his kingship.

The first major effort to negotiate with the French was made at a conference at Gravelines, just outside Calais, in 1439, an initiative that owed a great deal to Cardinal Beaufort, who led the English delegation. Beaufort received formal written instructions, detailing the very limited concessions he could offer to the French, including the release of the Duke of Orléans, the cousin of the French king and in English hands since his capture at Agincourt in 1415, but only for the enormous ransom of 100,000 marks. Four days after these written instructions were issued, however, Beaufort received secret instructions from Henry himself, in which the king set out his thoughts and intent regarding his title to the French crown. The secrecy around these instructions suggests that Henry was prepared to concede the use, though probably not the renunciation, of his title to the kingdom of France, concessions that would have been thoroughly unpopular with English public opinion. Beaufort was given full powers to negotiate on Henry's behalf, and after long and hard bargaining sent Henry back a draft agreement that contained a long-term truce in return for the cessation of Henry's use of his title of King of France, and the release of the Duke of Orléans without ransom. However, the council in England, led by Gloucester, could not accept these proposals and Henry, willingly or under pressure, refused the terms.

Nonetheless, within the year Henry had made the decision to free the Duke of Orléans – without ransom – in order that Orléans could use his influence with the French king to achieve a peace. After soliciting advice from his council on the pros and cons of releasing the duke, Henry not only decided to do so, but issued a statement via his council containing his reasoning, partly in response to the Duke of Gloucester's very public criticism of his actions. In his statement, Henry was emphatic that the responsibility for the decision lay with him and him alone: what had been done 'he hath done of himself and of his own advice and courage' and that he acted not 'of simpleness, nor of self-will' – interesting that he even needed to deny this – but for great and notable causes, some of which he had to keep secret, but some he could state.[2] There followed a long explanation of these latter reasons, which included a praiseworthy if naïve desire to bring peace to the bitterly divided Catholic Church and what, with hindsight, could be seen to be misdiagnoses of the state of politics in France and at the French court. The release of Orléans utterly failed to bring about Henry's hoped-for peace; indeed, it rather complicated the diplomatic situation, while the English had given up a substantial bargaining chip and foregone a sizeable ransom for nothing.

These failures meant that war would continue in the short term, and in 1441 Richard, Duke of York, was sent to Normandy with a substantial force to defend the duchy. Foolishly, however, some two years later Henry diverted men and resources from York to the sickly and incompetent Duke of Somerset, something he was probably persuaded to do by Cardinal Beaufort, who was Somerset's uncle. Somerset, ambitious for new conquests to expand his personal dominions in Maine, went to the defence of neither Normandy nor Gascony but, after a brief and ineffectual campaign in Maine and Anjou, returned home in disgrace and died shortly afterwards, perhaps by his own hand. Henry and Beaufort had shown poor judgement in their choice of commander and in their strategic targets, and it was the failure of this expensive expedition that caused the pendulum to swing again towards peace. Prosecuting the war after the failures of negotiation in 1439–40 was reasonable enough, but military setbacks meant that, when negotiations were resumed in 1444, England entered talks from a position not of strength, but of weakness.

Henry appointed a team of his intimate advisers, led by William, Earl of Suffolk, and Adam Moleyns, to conduct a fresh round of negotiations and, in another statement of his personal responsibility, made it a matter of record that the choice of Suffolk was his own and not made under the influence of anyone else – a highly unusual step. This time, however, negotiators were seeking not just peace or a truce with France, but also a wife for Henry. The talks resulted in an agreement for Henry to marry Margaret, daughter of René, Duke of Anjou, but the betrothal, solemnized by proxy on 24 May 1444, was accompanied only by a twenty-one-month truce with France and the promise of further negotiations. These occurred in London in the summer of 1445. The French ambassadors' accounts of the meeting have survived, and with them a pen-portrait of a friendly – perhaps excessively friendly – English king:

[Henry] came to the said ambassadors, and putting his hand to his hat and raising it from his head he said two or three times 'Saint Jehan, grant mercis; Saint Jehan, grant mercis' and took each of them by the hand behind backs.

When the ambassadors wished to leave the king 'said "no" and detained them, and he appeared to be pleased to see them, but he did not speak otherwise to them'.[3] Most of the practical negotiations were, as convention demanded, carried out by Suffolk and other close royal advisers. Nevertheless, the picture that emerges from this account is of Henry as a king fully engaged in the process. Moreover, his friendliness, in contrast with some of the others around the court, was a genuine personal effort to bring the French ambassadors on side.

During the summer 1445 talks, Henry agreed to cede English lands in Maine, conquered in the 1420s and which provided a key buffer zone to the south of Normandy. This was, in theory, to be a surrender to Henry's new father-in-law, René of Anjou, who was a subject of the King of France and whose territories of Anjou bordered Maine to the south. This concession was in return for a twenty-year truce between England and France. The agreement, deeply unpopular in England, was, so Henry later said, brought about through the personal intervention of his wife, René's daughter Margaret of Anjou.

On 22 December 1445 Henry wrote a letter to King Charles under his most personal seal, the signet, and added his sign-manual (signature), in which he promised to deliver all the English lands in Maine to René by April 1446, as this was 'one of the best and aptest ways to arrive at the blessing of a peace between us and you'.[4] While Henry could scarcely have written such a letter without his closest advisers, at the very least, being aware of what he was doing, the extraordinary naïvety of the concession as well as the personal authorization is clear evidence that this was the king's own initiative, the letter reinforcing the king's earlier oral proposal in the summer of 1445. Instead of the concession of Maine being conditional on a long-term peace – in itself an indication of the weakness of the English position – it was made merely in the hope that this would lead to peace. The handing-over of Maine was delayed until March 1448, in large part because of resistance by English commanders on the ground there, and was only completed because of the arrival of a large French army which took custody of the provincial capital of Le Mans – for Charles VII rather than René of Anjou. All the English achieved was a meagre extension of the truce until April 1450.

Henry's involvement in the inept English diplomacy that followed was less clear. English pressure on the Duke of Brittany, a vassal of France, to back the English in Normandy only drove him to appeal to King Charles VII who, just over a year after the truce extension was signed, attacked Normandy. Almost certainly, this was not Henry's doing – Suffolk was seen then and now as the primary agent of policy, and the Duke of Somerset was the military commander on the ground who lost Normandy in very little time – but Henry was, of course, ultimately responsible. It seems likely that he was advised that the maladroit machinations on the Breton borders, including the seizure of the Breton town of Fougères, would not lead to war, as this was neither Henry's personal inclination nor militarily sustainable. Yet it did, and what Henry V had taken several years to conquer was lost within one. England's unreadiness for the resumption of the war in France was matched by the government's failure to raise sufficient men and troops to save it. A small relief force, perhaps 2,500 men strong, was not enough to rescue Normandy, assaulted by French forces more than ten times the size, and was quickly and predictably defeated at the Battle of Formigny in April 1450, which set the seal on English losses in northern France. Only one figure could have led a major English rescue force, the only possible salvation for the crumbling province. Yet there seems to have been no discussion at any stage that Henry, aged twenty-eight and – in theory – in his prime, would accompany an English army to the rescue of his English and French subjects in Normandy.

The extent of Henry's direct involvement in the foreign policy of the realm in the 1440s has been questioned. As John Watts has pointed out, the repeated public pronouncements that a certain policy had been decided by Henry himself were highly unusual and should not have been necessary. Clearly, Henry was more than usually influenced by the men around him and, more damagingly, was perceived to be so by political society. At times, such as the disastrous – from the English perspective – French embassy of 1445, Suffolk seems to have been responsible for much that happened around the king, and perhaps even for the direction of policy. Yet to discount Henry entirely from the decision-making process seems a step too far. If Henry was open to the influence of those who sought peace in the 1440s – an entirely reasonable policy – such openness was surely due to the fact that he himself sought this end. Certain decisions, such as the surrender of Maine, could only be made by the king. While, inevitably, all the formal evidence suggests that Henry made these decisions on his own account, to discount the evidence on this basis, rather than accept it while acknowledging that others could and did have a role in the direction and implementation of policy, is unnecessary. Furthermore, private or off-the-record sources, such as the account of the French ambassadors, and most importantly the secret letters by Henry to Charles in which Maine was ceded, cannot be easily argued to show anything other than the king's intimate involvement with the direction of policy.

The speed of Lancastrian Normandy's collapse was matched only by that of the fall of Lancastrian Gascony. In 1449, preoccupied conquering Normandy, the French made only limited inroads into Gascony, but in autumn the following year a more substantial advance saw much greater progress, and the province's capital, Bordeaux, fell on 29 June 1451, with its second city, Bayonne, surrendering on 22 August. Long delays in raising money and troops meant an English military response did not come until a year later, in the summer of 1452; then, however, somewhat surprisingly, Bordeaux was retaken on 23 October 1452. The recovery was to be short-lived. A shattering English defeat at Castillon on 17 July 1453, the last battle of the Hundred Years War, ended English hopes, and Bordeaux was retaken that October. Henry VI and his government had lost Normandy, held for three decades, and Gascony, held for four centuries, within the space of just four years. An economic downturn, caused by bullion shortage and a decline in exports, financial exhaustion, war-weariness among both English taxpayers and the military classes, a dearth of capable commanders (with one or two honourable exceptions) and an increasing sense of national feeling which meant that many Normans and some Gascons were unwilling to co-operate with the English all contributed to the defeats. Yet inept diplomacy, poor strategic thinking, the precedence given from limited funds to religious foundations and the expanding royal household rather than the defence of Lancastrian France, and most of all the lack of royal leadership, were also major factors. Henry, ultimately responsible for his government's prioritization of domestic expenditure over overseas defence, and directly responsible for the failure to give military leadership, must take the lion's share of the blame.

There were also serious problems with Henry's governance of England, and the build-up of discontent with his rule erupted in violence in 1450. Henry's generosity to petitioners and his general profligacy had a major impact on government in the 1440s, both in terms of reduced income and in the administration of justice. In turn this brought down widespread opprobrium on his advisers. Justice was seen to be hindered by the king's interventions, and disorder exacerbated by his grants. For example, a royal pardon was granted to John Bolton in 1444 before his trial for the murder of a woman after an attempted rape. In parliament shortly afterwards, the Commons petitioned that he should be tried despite the pardon, arguing that the king had been ignorant of Bolton's crimes when the pardon was given. Another pardon was granted to

Lord Scrope and a number of his household men for the murder of a Suffolk esquire in 1446 on the grounds that they had been falsely accused by the victim's widow – despite the fact that they had been formally indicted before justices of the peace and two presenting juries, that no accusation had been made by the widow, and that Scrope had admitted that two of the men pardoned had actually committed the murder. In 1441, in the midst of a serious feud between the Earl of Devon and another south-western peer, Lord Bonville, Henry granted the office of the stewardship of the duchy of Cornwall, perhaps the most influential and important office in the south-west of England, to the Earl of Devon, despite the fact that Lord Bonville had held it since 1437. A week later Henry was forced to send an urgent letter to Devon not to take up the office until the council had met to discuss it, given that if Devon were to do so, violence would very likely follow. While the later 1430s and 1440s did not see anything like the level of violence and disorder that was to follow in the 1450s, contemporaries were aware of serious problems: one popular manifesto put it that 'the law serves of nought else in these days but for to do wrong, for nothing is sped almost except false matters by colour of the law for mede [reward or bribery], dread and favour, and so no remedy is had in the court of conscience in any way'.[5] It may have been something of an exaggeration – but it was a damning indictment nonetheless.

The origins of the problem with the English royal finances lay not with Henry, but rather in both the ongoing French war and the economic slump that was to worsen through the 1440s and 1450s. In 1433, during Henry's minority, the Lord Treasurer told parliament that the crown's ordinary revenues were £64,000, its foreseeable expenses in the following year £80,000 and that its debts had reached £165,000. The order of the day then, when Henry came of age, was to restrain expenditure and to economize. Yet, of course, Henry's priorities ran entirely counter to these imperatives. Not only were the royal foundations of Eton and King's expensive, both in terms of loss of royal lands given for their endowment and the ongoing building costs, but also the royal household became an even greater financial burden. In 1433 the adolescent Henry's household was estimated to cost £13,678 per year. This expenditure would inevitably rise a little as Henry emerged into adulthood, but few could have foreseen the extent to which it was to rise. Despite ordinances in 1445, which in vain sought to restrain Henry from adding to its already swollen numbers, by this time the king's household, having mushroomed in size, was now costing vast sums – perhaps £24,000 annually by 1450, when royal debts were alleged to have reached £372,000.

Another factor, albeit one incalculable with any degree of precision, also had a major impact. The flood of permanent and temporary grants of lands, offices and rents to servants, courtiers and others benefited the recipients at the expense of the crown: many, perhaps most, of these grants and leases were below the market rate, reducing the crown's income stream from rents and profits of landownership. Henry also granted more life annuities and made more permanent alienations of crown lands than most other kings. In short, Henry's liberality weakened the crown's already precarious financial position.

There was also a public perception that Henry's bounty was distributed mostly to those around him, who had access to him and could most easily influence him or place petitions before him, and that many of the men advanced and enriched were so favoured primarily because they were the king's intimates, rather than receiving just rewards for diligent service. These suspicions were right – at least in part. On one count, the number of grants to household servants was 123 in 1445–6, up from 59 in 1444–5. If the lesser men benefited, the great men around the king benefited more. Men like William Aiscough, one of the royal chaplains, whose meteoric rise through the ranks of the Church culminated in his becoming Bishop of Salisbury in 1439 and then royal confessor, was perceived as being so influential with Henry that he was able to interfere in the king's intimate relations with the queen. Aiscough had also amassed a substantial fortune in Henry's service: when in 1450 he was hacked to death by a mob, the goods he was travelling with (and which were taken by the mob) were said to be worth £4,000, twice the annual revenues of his bishopric.

Another man who profited greatly from Henry's profligacy was James Fiennes. The younger son of a Sussex knight, Fiennes rose to the dizzying heights of the peerage as Lord Say, having served Henry as chamberlain of the royal household and Lord Treasurer of England. More material reward followed, as he was granted the constableship of Dover Castle and an annuity of £200 per annum, as well as a host of other offices, prompting one historian to say he 'fed mightily at the trough of royal munificence'.[6] So unpopular did Fiennes become that he was removed from office by the concerted grievances of the Commons in parliament in 1450; later that year he was killed during the major popular uprising known as Cade's rebellion, after the (probable) name of one of its leaders, Jack Cade. Most notoriously, William de la Pole, Earl of Suffolk, effectively Henry's leading minister in the 1440s, benefited greatly from Henry's generosity in almost every way. Promoted to Marquess in 1444 and Duke of Suffolk in 1448, he reached the top rank of the peerage (a significant achievement for a man whose great-grandfather was a wool merchant from Hull). He successfully asked the king for custody of prize heiresses in the wardship of the crown, both to advance his family and so that he could exploit their estates, and in addition to grants of lands and privileges, he received a string of influential and lucrative offices.

These and other courtiers were loathed. Cade's rebels in 1450 described 'insatiable, covetous and malicious persons ... daily and nightly about his highness' who whenever 'anything should come to him by his laws, anon they ask it from him', as well as giving the king false advice and counsel.[7] Aiscough, Fiennes and Suffolk were all murdered by popular mobs in 1450, as was Adam Moleyns, Bishop of Chichester, another of the men who dominated the royal council. Others around the king, the court and the royal household were seen as legitimate targets for popular ire. Aiscough, Fiennes, Moleyns and Suffolk would, of course, have seen themselves as acting for the good of the country, and their promotion and the accumulation of (some) wealth as legitimate reward for their services – though it is harder to see how they would have justified the full extent of their accumulation of treasure. There have been recent attempts to rehabilitate Suffolk's reputation, arguing that his was not a corrupt court clique but a reasonably inclusive regime that fell apart only with the resumption of the French war in 1449 and the subsequent English collapse. There is a sense that these men were ultimately scapegoats for the failings of Henry, the man responsible for their promotion, accumulation of wealth, and the extent of their dominance of government. Yet, given their degree of control of government and policy in the 1440s, coupled with a concern to further their own interests which even Suffolk's most sympathetic historian has stated 'was, at the very least, indiscreet',[8] they must accept a degree of responsibility for the disasters that manifested themselves in the English state and its dominions in 1450.

Before the final loss of Normandy that year Henry VI and his government suffered a series of domestic shocks. The first was the fall of the king's principal minister, William de la Pole, Duke of Suffolk. Held responsible for the defeats in Normandy, he was impeached in the Commons, and accused of a wide range of crimes, foremost of which were treason and corruption. Although the accuracy of most of the accusations was questionable, to a large extent that was irrelevant – it was a mud-slinging exercise designed to damage and discredit. Indeed, while Suffolk was responding to the first set of allegations, the Commons, determined to get their man, brought more and more charges against him, making him responsible for all the disasters of the previous years. Yet Suffolk never came to trial. In the presence of the majority of the English peerage Henry, through his chancellor, declared Suffolk neither innocent nor convicted of the charges of treason, and banished him for five years – essentially for his own good. The lords probably did not disapprove of this decision. Not only were they keen that the Commons should not have the power to try peers of the realm, but many of them, at one time or another, had been party to decisions made for which Suffolk was being blamed.

Once again it is not quite clear how much the verdict was Henry's. Was he being loyal to a man he trusted and who he thought had served him well, or was he being influenced by those at his court, closely allied with Suffolk, who were trying to save their own skins by saving Suffolk from a trial – or was it, indeed, a combination of both? In the event Henry's concern availed Suffolk little. The ship taking him into exile was boarded by another English ship, whose sailors seized him, staged a mock trial and executed him, and on 2 May threw his body onto the Kentish shore.

Within weeks Kent was up in arms, demanding solutions for the problems of the realm. This blossomed into a major popular rebellion, something that had not happened in England for seventy years. Provoked in part by the defeat in Normandy, in part by the perception of the court clique as ruling the king for their own benefit, this was a genuine popular uprising that shook the nation. Nor was this simply a rising of the very poorest: gentlemen and esquires, the middling and higher end of county society, are known to have been involved. Their demands, indicative of the dire state of government in the realm, echoed those of the parliament of earlier that year: punishment of the traitors (the affinity and supporters of the Duke of Suffolk who had lost France), that all the king's grants be revoked (a 'resumption'), which would, in their eyes, solve his impoverishment by bringing back lucrative lands and offices into his own hands, and the ending of particular abuses in the law and local administration, with a strong focus on more local and specifically Kentish issues. There was no direct complaint against the king himself; his right to rule was not called into question by the rebels. This was not unusual; those around the king were always blamed, rather than the king himself, as to blame the king could be construed as treason. However, if the criticisms made by his parliament and the fact that many of his subjects were now up in arms were not sufficient to indicate the severity of the crisis, the royal army that had been gathered to crush the Kentish rebellion mutinied and refused to move against the rebels, instead taking up their cries for reform. Unlike the young Richard II, who in 1381 had personally confronted the leaders of the Peasants' Revolt, Henry fled, reaching his castle of Kenilworth in Warwickshire three weeks later. In the end Cade's rebels were defeated by the citizens of London, rather than a royal army, but not before a number of Henry's hated inner circle were killed.

Initially, Henry opted for clemency, offering pardons to many rebels; after Cade was seized and died in captivity the majority of his supporters returned home. Sporadic disorder, though, continued throughout the autumn of 1450 and 1451. In trying to suppress it, Henry and his government abandoned their policy of mercy, acting instead in a heavy-handed manner, executing many, particularly in Kent, where the judicial suppression was known as 'the harvest of heads'.[9] Having fled in the face of Cade's rebellion, leaving others to fight for him and suppress the rebellion, and then punished ongoing disturbance with excessive severity, Henry 'had handled rebellion at home as badly as he had previously managed the affairs of his French kingdom'.[10]

In the aftermath of Cade's rebellion, Richard Plantagenet, Duke of York, emerged as the chief opponent of Henry's government. Previously a loyal governor of France in 1436 and 1440–45, and then of Ireland until the autumn of 1450, York returned to England broadcasting to the whole realm both his loyalty to Henry VI and his plan for reform of the kingdom – a plan that was similar to, and therefore drew popular strength from, the demands of parliament and Cade's rebels. Arguing for a resumption of all the king's grants to re-establish the royal finances on a sound footing and punishment for the traitors around the king who had caused the loss of France, York saw himself in the position of the king's new chief minister. His programme was popular among the ordinary people, frustrated and increasingly seeking a voice in the realm, but not among the court and the majority of the peerage, who held the balance of power in the country. Instead of York, Edmund Beaufort, Duke of Somerset, fresh from losing Normandy, established himself as the king's leading minister in the spring of 1451: in doing so, he built on the late and unpopular Duke of Suffolk's power base within the court and royal household. Blamed by many of those on the ground in France for its loss, and held responsible by many in England, Somerset had little to commend him in becoming the most influential man at court and in government, and was certainly unacceptable to the leading critic of that administration, York. York's frustrations at the rejection of his programme and his pretensions to run the government boiled over. In 1452 he raised a rebellion in all but name at Dartford, but, faced with a substantial royal army, York was forced to submit to the king, and was thrown into the political wilderness.

The three years between the end of Cade's rebellion in 1450 and Henry's collapse in August 1453 are often said to have been the most active and most successful of Henry's reign. Some historians, indeed, suggest that he was finally growing into the role, motivated by the disasters of 1450; or perhaps, with the vacuum created by the deaths of Suffolk, Moleyns, Aiscough, Saye and others, he had more room to develop. These years, however, can only be described as successful in very limited terms. His one unqualified achievement was that after eight years of marriage, Queen Margaret became pregnant for the first and only time and, on 13 October 1453, gave birth to a healthy boy, christened Edward. It was also true that following the collapse of English Gascony in 1451, Henry was granted money by parliament and a substantial force was sent under the best English commander available, John Talbot, Earl of Shrewsbury, to recover the duchy, with surprising initial success. Henry was able to overcome the challenge of York in 1452, which, although it had been explicitly aimed at his leading courtiers, clearly sought to control him; its failure was in part the result of continuing noble loyalties to Henry himself, his unquestioned right to be on the throne, and York's political failings.

Yet for the most part, this active period of kingship comprised judicial tours around the south-east of England, in which Henry meted out severe, perhaps excessive, justice on those implicated in the rebellions by Cade and then York. Given the contrast with his usual leniency, Henry may have been advised and urged to be harsher in order to emphasize his authority. It was an approach that was hardly likely to endear Henry to his subjects, and later events were to see Kent and the south-east support the Yorkists rather than Henry's own dynasty. Punishments for York's supporters went a long way to hardening attitudes among York and his allies against Henry's inner circle, with fatal consequences for all concerned.

Nonetheless, in the summer of 1453 Henry was seemingly in a stronger position than he had been for a number of years. Aristocratic and popular opponents within his realm had been overcome, and as the loss of his French territories can only have been a source of devastating shame to him, efforts to recover Gascony at least appeared to be bearing fruit. Yet Fortune's wheel was about to turn once more, and cast him into the depths. Henry suffered a total mental collapse, one unparalleled in English medieval history, and from which he never fully recovered.

3
Collapse and Catastrophe,
1453–1461

In early August 1453, at the royal hunting lodge of Clarendon near Salisbury, Henry VI lost his senses. He would never fully recover them. The onset was sudden: one contemporary chronicle described how 'he fell, through a sudden and unexpected fright, into such an illness that for a full year and a half he was without natural sense or intelligence adequate to administer the government'.[1] The juxtaposition of this event and the receipt around this time of news of the defeat of the English army at Castillon in Gascony on 17 July, which doomed the recovery of the duchy, may well not have been a coincidence.

Usually referred to as the king's 'madness', Henry's symptoms did not require the medieval equivalent of a straitjacket; instead he was, for most of the next eighteen months, in a stupor or catatonic state. Two contemporary accounts illustrate the severity of the attack to which he had succumbed. About three months after his collapse and two months after the birth of his son in October 1453:

the Duke of Buckingham took him [the baby prince] in his arms and presented him to the King in goodly wise, beseeching the King to bless him; and the King gave no manner of answer. Nevertheless the Duke abode still with the Prince by the King; and when he could no manner answer have, the Queen came in, and took the Prince in her arms and presented him in like form as the Duke had done, desiring that he should bless it; but all their labour was in vain, for they departed thence without any answer or countenance, saving only that once he looked on the Prince and caste down his eyes again, without any more.[2]

Two months later, in a last-ditch attempt to rouse the king, a delegation of lords went to him at Windsor to discuss urgent business, but, reported one of their number, the Bishop of Coventry and Lichfield, 'they could get no answer nor sign, for no prayer nor desire, lamentable cheer nor exhortation, nor anything that they or any of them could do or say, to their great sorrow and discomfort'. Later they asked for the king to be moved, 'and so he was led between two men into the Chamber where he lies', but again they could get no response.[3] Abbot Whethamstede of St Albans, who may not have been an eyewitness, nonetheless provides a description that fits closely with this picture, noting that Henry had lost his memory and control of his limbs, being unable to walk or move without help from where he was seated.

With such scraps of information, it is difficult to produce a definitive modern medical diagnosis. The condition most often ascribed to Henry is catatonic schizophrenia: a state, often brought on by a stressful episode, in which the subject experiences extreme loss of motor ability. It is also

1. A contemporary depiction of the descent of the crowns of France (left) and England (right) culminating in Henry VI (bottom), showing his formidable but challenging inheritance.

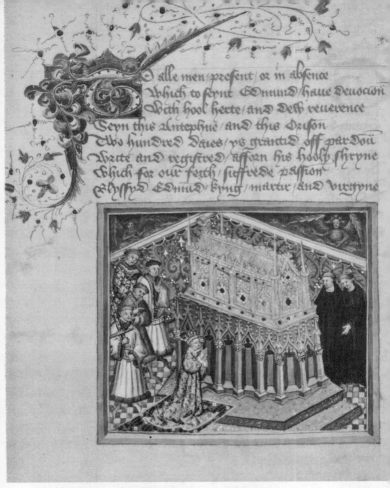

O alle men present, or in absence
Which to seynt Edmund haue deuocion
With hool herte, and deuli reuerence
Seyn this Antephne, and this Orison
Two hundred Daies, ys grauntid off pardon
Write and registred, afforn his hooly shryne
Which for our feith, suffrede passion
Blyssyd Edmund kyng, martir, and virgyne

2. A miniature of the young Henry VI praying at the shrine of King Edmund at Bury St Edmunds, probably reflecting his visit there in 1433 when he was twelve.

3. Henry's English bible is further evidence of his religious interests. It was a highly unusual item for a king to own at this date, since the English Church in 1407–8 had banned the translation on which this was based, as it was associated with a heretical movement. The note in the second column is later evidence for his ownership.

This section is from the Book of Revelation, Chapter XXII (noted on the second line), describing St John's vision of the heavenly Jerusalem.

4. Illuminated miniature of Henry VI praying in the
foundation charter of King's College, Cambridge, 1441.

5. Henry's two great educational and religious foundations: Eton College, Berkshire (above) and King's College, Cambridge (below).

6. Henry's posthumous saintly reputation is reflected in the high number of pilgrim badges found in England, mainly in the south. The king holds an orb and sceptre, with a fantastical antelope (a badge used by him during his lifetime) at his feet.

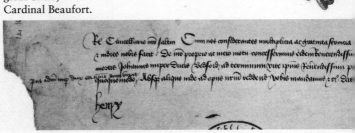

7. This is the only known example of Henry's full signature, on a document dated 28 July 1436, when he was just fifteen, granting land to his great-uncle, Cardinal Beaufort.

8. The royal sign manual ('R H' for Rex Henricus) shows considerable variation in the later 1450s. Evidence of Henry's shaky hand or possibly of forgery?
Top left, March 1458;
top right, January 1458;
left, December 1459.

9. Henry has added in his own handwriting a note on a formal royal grant that the grant was his pious gift ('alms') to St John of Bridlington, a saint whose cult had strong Lancastrian connections.

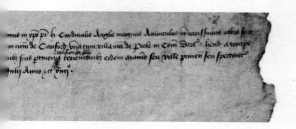

10. Screen painting of Henry VI in the chancel of the south chapel at Barton Turf (Norfolk), probably dating from the late 1480s or 1490s. The label reads 'Rex Henricus Sextus' (King Henry VI); he is not directly described as a saint.

hereditable, perhaps between 40 and 80 per cent of the time. Henry's maternal grandfather, Charles VI of France, had lost his mind in 1392, though in a rather different way. Under physical stress (rather than the mental strain that seems to have triggered Henry's collapse), Charles became violent, killing four men of his household before he could be restrained; he continued to suffer breakdowns throughout his life. Henry's great-grandmother, Charles's mother, also appears to have suffered a breakdown aged thirty-five – 'losing her good sense and her good memory'[4] – although she apparently recovered after a few months, living another five years. It seems very likely that Henry's mental weakness was inherited from his maternal ancestors.

No adult king of England before this date had ever fully lost his mental faculties, and consequently his ability to rule, in so comprehensive a manner. The nearest equivalent was Edward III, who appears to have been mentally and physically debilitated by a series of strokes by the end of his life, but was still nominally in control of government even if heavily influenced by a clique around him. Clearly Henry could not be considered to be in any sort of control. In the circumstances, it is astonishing that it took eight months before any formal solution to the problem was found, thus reflecting the difficulty and gravity of the situation, the absence of a member of the immediate royal family who could take over, and the factional fault lines within the English nobility. Although marginalized after the failure of his 'loyalist' rebellion in 1452, without the king the political isolation of Richard, Duke of York, the most powerful magnate and unofficially next in line to the throne after the infant Prince Edward, was unsustain-able. If York was to be brought in from the political wilderness, then he was really the only choice to govern in the king's stead, and he was eventually appointed Protector of England on 27 March 1454. If York was in, then his political rival, the Duke of Somerset, was out, and was imprisoned in the Tower for nearly a year, though the sub-stantial body of moderate magnates who held the balance of power prevented York from bringing him to trial for the loss of Normandy. While historians have debated just how parti-san York's protectorship was, there is some agreement that it did provide a period of stable government, despite the uncertainty over how long it would last and how far Henry might recover, if he ever did.

Henry is generally believed to have been in this cata-tonic stupor for one and a half years, but this is not quite the whole picture. There were moments where the king, appearing in public, was able to give at least the superficial impression that he was functioning normally. The East Anglian gentleman William Paston, writing from London to his brother John in Norfolk on 6 September 1454, described how the Archbishop-elect of Canterbury had made his formal submission to the king, and received his cross of office in return: 'My Lord of Canterbury has received his cross, and I was with him in the king's cham-ber when he made his homage. I told Harry Wylton the demeaning between the king and him; it was too long to write.'[5] While it is frustrating that the king's behaviour (his 'demeaning') is not described, the fact that it was a topic that was too long to commit to paper probably indicates that the king had not recovered that far mentally, even if physically he was able to move about. Nonetheless, homage was a formal and solemn public act, and if his recovery was still very limited it is surprising that he was allowed or even able to appear. Henry's occasional public appearances (we know of two) must have created more uncertainty than is usually acknowledged for those trying to run the country, particularly Protector York. However, the suspicion that Henry had not made anything approaching a full recovery when he received the Archbishop of Canterbury in September 1454 is confirmed by another of John Paston's correspondents, writing on 9 January 1455, and describing Henry making a sudden and apparently complete recovery at the Christmas recently passed:

> Blessed be God, the King is well amended, and has been since Christmas day . . . and on the Monday afternoon the Queen came to him, and brought my Lord Prince with her. And then he asked what the Prince's name was, and the Queen told him Edward . . . and he said he never knew until that time, nor knew not what was said to him, nor knew where he had been whilst he had been sick until now. And my Lord of Winchester and my Lord of Saint John's were with him on the morrow after Twelfthday [7 January], and he spoke to them as well as he ever did; and when they came out they wept for joy.[6]

The tears of joy would soon dry. As one historian put it: 'If Henry's insanity had been a tragedy, his recovery was a national disaster.'[7]

Henry's recovery at Christmas 1454 inevitably brought York's protectorate to an end. But the implication by contemporaries that Henry had made a full recovery is questionable. Despite apparently being 'well amended', he signed no government documents before 8 April 1455, and only twenty-five between then and the following November, a significant contrast with his annual average of around 180 in the 1440s.[8] Thus the problem of what happened over the next few months, as so frequently with Henry VI, is one of the king's agency. Step by step, Somerset resumed his former position as the leading figure in the government (an Italian writer in London noted 'my lord of Somerset ruled as usual'),[9] while York and his allies lost power and office, and moves were made against them that might – to them – appear to be hostile. It is simply not clear whether this was Henry's conscious policy, whether he merely slipped back into the habits of reliance on Somerset and the key members of his household, or whether his recovery was limited enough for those around him to manoeuvre him in order to benefit themselves. But, however it happened, giving Somerset back the reins of government and moving against York was not a prudent policy, and did not go unpunished.

Summoning a great council to meet in late May at Leicester, where the disputes between York and Somerset were to be resolved – with the great likelihood that the latter would have much the better of any settlement – the king left London on 21 May and moved north with a respectable following. But York and his key allies, the Neville Earls of Warwick and Salisbury, took matters into their own hands. Warwick and Salisbury were themselves at odds with Somerset over the ownership of the lordship of Glamorgan, and in the midst of a bitter local struggle with the Percy family for dominance of the north; this struggle had already erupted in bloodshed at the Battle of Heworth in August 1454, and the conflict between these two powerful families was increasingly important in local and national politics. With a larger and better-armed force of perhaps 3,000 men, York, Warwick and Salisbury marched swiftly south, proclaiming their loyalty in letters to the king but also making demands for 'justice' against Somerset. The royal force stopped at St Albans, the first major town on the road north from London, on the evening of 21 May, and reinforcements were summoned, but York's army arrived first.

At this crucial juncture, trapped and outnumbered by a 'rebel' army, King Henry delegated full responsibility for negotiation with his rebellious leading subjects to the Duke of Buckingham; it was later alleged that York's letters containing his demands had not even been shown to him. Placing Buckingham rather than Somerset in charge seems to have been one of those occasional assertions of royal will, as Buckingham was a less polarizing and odious figure to the Yorkist lords than Somerset, yet Henry's refusal to engage in person in the process of negotiating with several of his most important and dangerous subjects was a shocking abdication of personal responsibility. Henry presumably held the naïve belief that the Yorkists would not actually attack the royal force, by then sheltering behind barricades in St Albans. This was a mistake: the Yorkists, frustrated by the fruitless negotiations and presumably thinking that they had had to complete the risky task they had set themselves before royal reinforcements arrived, attacked the town.

During the years of crisis in English-held France, up until the complete loss of English territories there in 1453, Henry had never led a royal army to France. Instead, on 22 May 1455 his first experience of battle was against his own subjects; it was to be a traumatic and disastrous one. Breaking through the barricades, the Yorkists targeted the noblemen around the king. Somerset, the Earl of Northumberland, the head of the Percy family, and his ally Lord Clifford were killed, Buckingham and Henry himself were wounded, and the king, deserted by his men and left alone, took refuge in the house of a tanner.[10] Henry himself was unlikely to have been a target for the rebels – killing him would have caused York and his allies more problems than solutions – though this may not have been obvious to Henry, fleeing a shower of arrows and watching his household men cut down around him. Henry's wound, in the neck, was clearly not deemed too serious, and he was fit to receive York, Warwick and Salisbury as his loyal liege men in the abbey at St Albans the same day. York and his allies now had possession of the king, and, having eliminated their rivals, including Somerset, were now in control of the government.

Although the wound he received at St Albans was apparently quickly treated, there are hints that it had a longer-term impact, that it retarded or reversed Henry's questionable recuperation from his mental breakdown.

His curious passivity before the battle might be an indication that his recovery from mental illness was limited, but some years later, in the autumn of 1457, an approver (an accomplice to a felony who turned king's evidence) repeated a treasonable conversation in which one Robert Burnet stated that the king 'sleepeth too much therto he was hurt at Saint Albans, would God he had been hurt so that he could never rise'.[11] The reason this evidence cannot just be dismissed as idle chatter is that both the speaker and his listener were yeomen of Westminster: while it is not possible to identify them as men of the royal household, their residence near the epicentre of government there makes it feasible that this gossip came from an informed source. Within a fortnight of the battle, Henry was sick again, perhaps a partial relapse of his mental illness brought on by the shock of the mêlée; a distinguished physician (rather than a battlefield surgeon), summoned on 5 June, was presumed to know the nature of his illness. Henry's health remained an issue for much of the summer, and in late October one correspondent of the Paston family, whose surviving letters do so much to illuminate the politics of these years, wrote that 'some men are afraid that he is sick again'.[12]

Uncertainty over the king's health continued, but there is no incontrovertible evidence that the king had a major relapse in the summer or autumn of 1455. Yet despite this, the Duke of York was appointed Protector of the Realm for the second time. Previously Protectors had only ever been appointed when the king was absent from the realm or clearly unable to rule. In contrast the second protectorate is explained by York's political ascendancy after his victory at St Albans. Parliament had assembled on 9 July, and sat until prorogued on 31 July, during which time York had pushed through royal pardons for himself and his allies for their actions at St Albans, appointed his supporters and friends to key posts, and begun to make moves to fulfil his reform programme for royal government. The programme, embracing attempts to restore law and order and royal finance, and seek justice on those who had been leading the king astray, was a tall order, but York was bound by his repeated public pronouncements on these topics to attempt to undertake them. When parliament reconvened in November 1455, the Lords agreed to York becoming Protector for a second time. The terms of this appointment were almost identical to those of his first, when the king was in a state of prostration; and York's protectorate could only be ended when Henry VI's son came of age, at least fifteen years away, or if the king came in person to parliament to relieve York of his office, with the advice of the lords spiritual and temporal.

Part of the reason for York's appointment was the dire state of the realm. A resumption of private warfare in the north between the Nevilles and Percies ended in a Neville victory at Stamford Bridge on 31 October, and a new outbreak of violent feuding in the West Country between the Earl of Devon and Lord Bonville, which saw a battle at Clyst on 15 December – which meant that the country was in urgent need of strong government. Accordingly the House of Commons petitioned that York be made Protector.

This appointment was not explicitly justified on the

grounds of Henry's health but on his incapacity to rule. On 11 November a great council, at which York was not present, concluded that the king was not able to preside over the new parliamentary session in person. Nothing explicit was said in the address to the Commons the following day about Henry's health – just that 'for certain just and reasonable causes' he was unable to attend – and the Commons, requesting the appointment of the Protector, noted that the king 'might not personally hereafter attend to the defence of this land', as such business must be 'over grievous and tedious to his Highness'.[13]

Yet one wonders about Henry's health during this time. If it was simply a question of York wanting to sideline Henry and rule as Protector, it seems strange that he waited until the second session of parliament in November, rather than pushing the act through parliament as soon as it met in July, not long after his victory at St Albans. There is very limited evidence of Henry's engagement with government between April and November 1455. Yet it took three months after the dissolution of the protectorate on 25 February 1456 before the king signed a warrant or council minute on 12 May (some warrants were passed by the king himself to the Lord Chancellor from 2 March). The fact that essential business could be portrayed by the Commons as grievous and tedious to the king suggests an acknowledgement by the political elite that Henry's recovery was limited, and had perhaps been set back by the trauma of his wounding at St Albans; for all York's political ascendancy, it was Henry's weakened state that made the second protectorate possible.

The end of York's protectorate did not, unlike the end of the first, appear to have been dependent on improvements in the king's health. Rather, it stemmed from York's failure to gather enough support to push through the centrepiece of his reforms, an Act of Resumption revoking many of Henry's grants of land and office, which would impact negatively on many individuals, such as the queen and Henry's Tudor half-brothers, and institutions such as Eton and King's, but would significantly improve royal finances. That failure ensured that a majority of the lords in parliament backed the ending of his protectorate in February 1456. However, the end of York's protectorate also marked the end of effective government under Henry VI. Over the next five years, the political elite descended into factionalism and, ultimately, civil war.

Henry's weakness was the root of the political tension and turmoil after 1455. Before 1453 he was a king who, if only intermittently engaged with policy and decisions, nevertheless could and did engage. After 1455 contemporaries perceived that he was not ruling as he had done before, and the resulting uncertainty was a major cause of the collapse into civil war. A king whose health was fragile, the extent of whose recovery from an unparalleled mental collapse was uncertain, who could be sidelined by more forceful political players and to whom the business of kingship was 'over grievous and tedious' was a problem the political community had to face. While, when it suited his supporters, Henry could be portrayed as an active king, a ruler whose knightly courage caused York to capitulate in 1452, who had endured the rigours of a campaign in 1459, full of the 'spirit of wisdom of God' – such a portrayal was never entirely convincing.[14] Yet, and most importantly, his legitimacy as king was accepted by almost all until well after the outbreak of civil war; they fought over who should have control over him. It was only after five bloody battles between 1459 and early 1461 that the Yorkist faction was able to claim, with any chance of success, that Henry should be replaced.

Delving beneath the political propaganda to find Henry's real state in these last few years is harder even than in the period before his collapse. Authoritative evidence is almost non-existent, and chronicles, often written significantly after the event and under a Yorkist king, become increasingly partisan. We are forced to rely upon scraps of information from interested observers, and the records of the royal administration, which generally give conflicting representations of King Henry VI. Differing pictures from the evidence have led historians to reach differing conclusions about the state of Henry's mental health and his fitness to rule, with views ranging from 'a pathetic shadow of a king' to 'a king with decided opinions'.[15]

It is clear that after the end of York's second protectorate Henry was able to walk, talk and play some public role. Henry made a speech and engaged in conversation when receiving French ambassadors in 1456, and at his entry into Coventry on 16 August 1457 he 'gave the mayor and his brethren and all the commons by his own mouth rehearsed great thanks'.[16] Earlier in the year, meanwhile, Henry and his queen went in procession around Coventry, crowned and in great state.[17] Some vivid eyewitness descriptions (albeit made nearly forty years later) show Henry in action. On more than one occasion in the late 1450s he visited Westminster Abbey to plan the location of his tomb. Having identified a site, he then in person commanded a mason to mark out the length and breadth of his tomb. Yet in their informal accounts, the witness statements also show a more troubled and diffident king. When the abbot suggested that it would be appropriate for Henry to be buried in a chapel alongside his father, the king replied: 'Nay let him alone: he lieth like a noble prince, I will not trouble him.'[18] Perhaps he did not consider himself worthy of lying alongside his father. Instead, all the witnesses agreed that he intended to be buried next to Henry III, ironically enough a pious king whose reign was troubled by civil strife. One of these witnesses was John Ashby, clerk of the signet, a man who must have spent much time in Henry's presence. He described how, while Henry was still looking for the best position for his tomb within the abbey, various suggestions were made, to each of which the king made no answer. Presumably in veiled exasperation at his silence, some of the people accompanying Henry said to him:

> 'Sir this is the first time that you have anything done in this matter, we think it best that upon a better deliberation you determine your mind therein.' To the which the said King Henry gave answer in effect 'I hold that well done.'[19]

This intimate depiction of a king, either unable to make up his mind or unable to speak it, and needing to be managed by those around him, is striking.

Other evidence from the last few years of the reign also depicts a king withdrawn from the troubles of his realm. In 1460, he visited Crowland Abbey in Lincolnshire. Despite the ongoing political turmoil the Prior of Crowland, writing his chronicle, observed that 'here he stayed, in the full enjoyment of tranquillity, three days and as many nights, taking the greatest pleasure in the observance of his religious duties, and most urgently praying that he might be admitted into the brotherhood of our monastery'.[20] This was hardly the dynamic, active king of royal propaganda: rather the pious king with his eyes upon heaven, but more passive, limited and weakened than he had been for most of his long reign.

Nor, after 1455, was he even perceived as the leading member of the royal family. Henry had always been seen by critics as being too receptive to, and overly reliant on, the counsel of his ministers. Yet after York's second protectorate had come to an end, people started to focus increasingly on the role of Henry's undeniably active queen, Margaret of Anjou, to the exclusion of her husband. Sources that do so have to be treated with some caution: the queen, female and French, was naturally vulnerable to hostile comments in the misogynistic and xenophobic world of late-medieval England, and it was easier to blame her for the troubles than it was to attribute them to her husband – direct criticism of the king was always dangerous. However, these wide-ranging sources, written for both public and private consumption, together present a convincing picture that is hard to ignore. The Chancellor of Oxford University, Dr Thomas Gascoigne, writing in 1457 and thus strictly contemporary, noted that after York had been dismissed from the protectorship the queen 'dragged' the king to her houses in the county of Chester, from where she ruled.[21] Meanwhile, the anonymous writer of the chronicle known as the *Brut* commented that 'every lord in England at this time dared not disobey the Queen, for she ruled peaceably all that was done about the King, which was a good, simple and innocent man'.[22]

By 1461, with Henry deposed and the new Yorkist king, Edward IV, on the throne, writers were freed from the need not to criticize the reigning king and the verdicts on Henry and his kingship are damning. For the Crowland chronicler, writing after 1461 but having observed him at first-hand in 1460, 'in consequence of a malady that had been for many years increasing upon him, he had fallen into a weak state of mind'.[23] Bishop George Neville, admittedly an opponent and the brother of the Earl of Warwick, one of the leading Yorkist lords, described him as 'that puppet of a king' and a 'statue of a king' in a letter of April 1461.[24] Pope Pius II, presumably on information received from his legate in England, Francesco Coppini, who was excessively inclined towards the Yorkists, described Henry as 'more timorous than a woman, utterly devoid of wit or spirit'.[25] Even allowing for the pro-Yorkist perspectives of such works, these judgements on Henry are devastating.

Yet a different picture is, perhaps inevitably, painted by the sources of the royal administration between 1455 and 1460, one that apparently shows Henry actively involved in the government of the realm. A rather different image of Henry in the last few years of his reign can thus be constructed. Many of the chronicle accounts are problematic, and, using the procedural records behind the king's grants and decisions, the warrants for the Great Seal, it is possible to argue that they record decisions genuinely being made by the king.[26]

Documents could be authorized by fifteenth-century kings in a number of different ways. Many were simply passed to the senior officials as granted without alteration, and a later endorsement added by a clerk. However, kings could also show their approval by sealing the document with their signet, kept normally by their secretary, or even by writing on the documents themselves. Late-medieval kings rarely signed documents with their full names, but did add their initials – R (for 'Rex') and the first letter of their first name – known as the sign manual. This was a practice seen only intermittently before Henry's reign, but one that became frequent after he came of age in 1436: as discussed above, it is direct evidence that governmental business was placed before him for approval. Should the many documents on which Henry added his sign manual not be accepted as the king's decisions? There are at least a dozen examples after 1455 where the king's personal wishes were also added to his authorization, as had happened occasionally prior to 1453, such as that on a petition asking for the goods of a deceased man in 1458. A note was added to the petition by one of the king's attendants: 'the king wills that the said John have the one half of the goods of the foresaid Adam for the good service that he hath done unto the king and that the other half be brought to the Treasurer of his chamber and from thence to be delivered and be distributed in alms among the poor people'.[27] This characteristically pious gesture seems authentic and very much in keeping with examples from before the king's collapse.

However, the overall picture after 1453 is not so clear-cut. There are only a dozen or so examples where the king's personal wishes have been added to such documents – not so big a sample over seven years, and evidence only of Henry's occasional interventions with specific cases, several of which might in any case be characterized as pious or charitable gestures in keeping with his occasional decisions before 1450. With the rest of the warrants authorized by the royal sign manual, meanwhile, there are several problems. Given Henry's suggestibility, can we be sure that these decisions were actually his? It is very rarely recorded who was present when Henry signed these documents, but the king would never have been alone. There is no direct evidence that the documents put before Henry were pre-vetted but, then again, no such evidence could possibly have survived. If Henry was, in effect, rubber-stamping decisions, putting his mark where he was told to, was he actually ruling? Or was he merely a source of authority which others used for their varied purposes?[28] It is, besides, worth questioning whether all of the signatures on these documents were indeed Henry's. The sign manual in his last few years shows a considerable variation in letter forms as well as in the quality of their execution (see plate 8). This is most likely a result of Henry's variable health affecting his penmanship rather than forgery by those around him, but the latter cannot entirely be ruled out.

Another type of document, which with other kings is seen as a sign of personal involvement, is equally problematic as evidence of Henry's participation in decision-making. There are a small number of warrants authorized after 1454 by the signet. The same problem – the extent to which he was being managed – applies to the signet warrants as to those authorized by the sign manual, but there is an additional issue. Assuming that the sign manual was indeed Henry's, he had to be well enough to sign his name. With the signet, however, he did not: it could be used by somebody else on his behalf. There is at least one signet letter written in October 1453, well after Henry's collapse and before any hint of recovery, of which he cannot have had any knowledge.[29]

Then there is the volume of business apparently carried out by Henry in person. Between March 1456, after the end of the second protectorate, and the Battle of Northampton in July 1460 when Henry was captured by the Yorkists, there are 600 warrants for the Great Seal in the sequence for signed bills, an annual rate of 139.[30] This was a lower rate than earlier in the reign: in the regnal year between September 1445 and August 1446, Henry authorized 189 warrants, in that between September 1448 and August 1449, 184 were signed (though admittedly there was probably less business passing through the chancery in the later 1440s as government shrank in the face of political tension and then civil war). This was not a heavy workload, averaging a bill approximately every three days. Furthermore, the bills the king signed reflect only a fraction of the business a king did or ought to deal with – several thousand grants came out of the royal chancery each year, and they cannot be used as incontrovertible evidence of a king in control of the decision-making process.

The personal decision-making of any other medieval king, as evidenced in the signed bills, would not be questioned, and indeed this study has used similar evidence before 1453 to argue for Henry's involvement with government, at least in a limited way. However, the case of Henry VI is different, certainly after his collapse. No other medieval king had such demonstrably serious mental health issues; no other king was so notoriously susceptible to those around him; no other king was so clearly uninterested in the business of government. Furthermore, while each of these documents signed by the king was important to the recipient, they were not key decisions of national policy but generally minor matters of patronage. The most important questions were decided not by the king on paper but in council, parliament or just with his closest advisers behind closed doors. In other words, there were plenty of opportunities for the key figures to manage, cajole or force the king to do as they wished. This is particularly true after Henry's capture at the Battle of Northampton in 1460, when he seems to have acquiesced meekly to everything required of him. Indeed, he was in Yorkist hands for eight months before being recaptured by his wife's troops at the second Battle of St Albans; during this time he had declined, when asked, to make any case for why he ought to stay on the throne rather than being displaced by his rival Richard of York, and in fact had meekly accepted the compromise eventually agreed which disinherited his own son, then a small boy, in favour of York as heir to the English throne.

It is not possible to make a truly accurate assessment of Henry's mental or physical state after his madness. Probability and plausibility are the highest levels to which it is possible to aspire. The sources are thin, frequently lacking in insight, often with a not-so-subtle agenda, or, in the case of administrative documents, following formulae designed to hide authorship, initiative, direction and policy behind the impenetrable veil of royal authority. Yet what is opaque to the modern reader at the distance of half a millennium and with recalcitrant sources was not to some contemporaries. The great majority of Henry's subjects would never have seen him; most of those who did would have glimpsed Henry only from a distance on state occasions, when he could be stage-managed. But the great lords – the Dukes of York and Somerset, the Earls of Salisbury and Shrewsbury, Warwick and Wiltshire, to whom access to the king's person could not be denied – would have seen and spoken to the king in audience, in council and in private, and would have witnessed first-hand what mental damage had been wrought, and the extent of his recovery. This knowledge must have impacted on their decisions; that those decisions tended to be violent and made without much reference to Henry himself is telling. He was not fit enough to rule but fit enough not to be entirely discounted.

What can be seen of Henry as king from the politics of the last five years of the reign, from the end of the second protectorate in February 1456 to the climactic Battle of

Towton in March 1461? The most obvious point emerging from any study of the period before the actual outbreak of war in September 1459 is the sheer inconsistency of royal policy. In 1455 and 1456 Richard of York was treated with some respect; even before the dissolution of his protectorate one contemporary reported that 'the King, as it was told me by a great man, would have him chief and principal councillor'.[31] During the late 1450s several of his allies remained in key posts, and most strikingly, when the King of Scots invaded northern England in May 1456, it was to York that Henry entrusted an army to resist him. There were alternative candidates – the Duke of Buckingham was the wealthiest peer after York himself, had royal blood and military experience in France, and was a political moderate and acceptable to all sides – yet it was York who was chosen, who marched north, and who missed out on the opportunity for military glory when James II of Scotland left Northumberland for his own soil in face of the advancing English.

However, by that autumn, York and his allies were summoned to a council, where they were upbraided for their actions at St Albans the previous year and forced to swear an oath on the gospels and give a signed undertaking that they would do nothing to endanger the safety of the king or kingdom. Humiliating as these actions were, they must also have worried York and his Neville allies, Richard, Earl of Salisbury and his son Warwick 'the Kingmaker', that they were no longer safe from reprisals for their actions at St Albans. Yet, having alienated the Yorkists by such actions, another policy was put in place by autumn

1457 when there were moves towards a general reconciliation, culminating in the so-called Loveday of March 1458 when the two factions walked in procession through London to St Paul's Church, York walking hand in hand with Henry's Queen Margaret of Anjou, Salisbury with Somerset, in apparent amity, though the Yorkists had also been forced to agree to pay reparations to the heirs of the nobles killed by Yorkist troops at St Albans. Shortly afterwards, however, the king and queen returned to the Midlands, where Margaret began military preparations, gathering a force known to chroniclers as the 'queen's gallants' in order to defend her family. In June 1459 a great council was called to Coventry; York and the Nevilles were either not invited or, presumably in some fear for their safety, chose not to attend. In their absence they were accused of treason. York, Warwick and Salisbury, finding themselves faced with open hostility, sought to join forces, but Salisbury, marching from Middleham in Yorkshire to the Welsh border, was intercepted and attacked by Lancastrian forces. Despite being outnumbered, he defeated the queen's men at Blore Heath in Staffordshire on 23 September 1459. If the first Battle of St Albans in 1455 is usually seen as the beginning of the civil war, Blore Heath marked the opening of the most intensive and bloody period of the entire Wars of the Roses.

From employment to alienation to reconciliation to hostility within three years, the crown's policy towards the Yorkist lords was changeable and unpredictable. This was surely not the work of an active king making decisions, but of a king who was a puppet of different factions around him. Contemporaries clearly identified the queen as the most prominent influence around Henry: one chronicler 'knew well that all the workings that were done grew by her, for she was more wittier than the king'.[32] A number of noblemen, including the young Duke of Somerset, but also the Earls of Shrewsbury and Wiltshire and Viscount Beaumont, were closely associated with the queen, and were frequently at the king's court in the Midlands. Yet this group remained just a faction until 1459, and whenever there was a larger gathering of lords at great councils, the queen's outright hostility to York and the Nevilles was usually neutralized by the mass of the peerage, who did not want open conflict. It is surely in the interplay of these two groups that the inconsistency of policy can be found. As those who knew him or had access to him realized that Henry could not rule, the knowledge of the king's incapacity can only have confirmed the need to exert control, to defeat political opponents and to look to the good of the nation as a whole, however they perceived that to be exercised best. Queen Margaret sought to maximize royal authority and use the lands held directly by the crown, particularly in Cheshire, Lancashire and parts of the Midlands, to provide a basis for power; York and his allies tried to become the king's leading ministers, while marginalizing him and ruling through constitutional means in a protectorate; the bulk of the peerage sought good governance through noble unity and compromise under the king's authority. From all these viewpoints the king was a figurehead but little more.

None of these competing policies was ultimately

successful. The last eighteen months of the reign saw out-right war. There were seven battles (including the rout of the Yorkists at Ludford Bridge, where there was little fighting), and Henry was captured twice, firstly by the Yorkists at Northampton in July 1460 and then by the Lancastrians at the second Battle of St Albans in 1461. He seems to have been no more than a passive spectator at those battles where he was present: at Northampton he was captured in his tent, at St Albans he was allegedly found sitting under a tree, singing. By the time of the huge, bloody and decisive battle outside the Yorkshire village of Towton in March 1461, Henry was not even on the battlefield with the men who were fighting in his name. Instead he was with his wife and son ten miles away at York. In the end the solution to Henry's inability to rule was found: rather than ruling through him, he was to be replaced.

Richard of York had always had a latent claim to the throne that was arguably better than Henry's. In late 1460 he put forward his claim in parliament, though to general consternation, even from his allies. In the end the claim was fudged, with Henry allowed to keep his throne but York made his heir, disinheriting Prince Edward, in an act known as the Accord. York's personal quest to wear the English crown was ended by his death at the Battle of Wakefield a few weeks later, but he left a son, the eighteen-year-old Edward, Earl of March, to succeed him. Edward won his first battle at Mortimer's Cross in February 1461 over Welsh Lancastrians, but Henry was recaptured at the second Battle of St Albans two weeks later as Queen Margaret's army defeated the Earl of

Warwick. In returning (or being returned) to his wife and allies, the Yorkists argued, in a rather legalistic way, that Henry had broken the Accord made between York and himself in parliament, which all the lords present had sworn to uphold. York's son Edward thus felt able to proclaim himself king, and it was as King Edward IV that he led the Yorkist army at the Battle of Towton, on 29 March. The state of Henry's broken realm, split politically, dynastically and geographically between north and south, was uniquely evident as perhaps 50,000 Englishmen fought each other all day in a snowstorm in a battle of unparalleled savagery. Contemporaries claimed that 28,000 men died; even if a more realistic estimate of 9,000 is accepted, it was still the bloodiest battle on English soil until the civil war of the seventeenth century. Edward's victory turned Henry, over the next decade, successively into a fugitive, a prisoner, a puppet, and finally a victim of murder.

Conclusion
Death and Afterlife

After the disaster of Towton, Henry, Margaret and Prince Edward (who had all been in nearby York rather than on the battlefield itself) crossed the border to safety in Scotland. In what was to be a decade of turmoil for the Lancastrians, it was Margaret who seems to have made all the major decisions, even during the first three years when Henry was at liberty. It was Margaret who appealed for aid from her French compatriots and who travelled to France to secure French troops in 1462; it was Margaret with whom English conspirators were in correspondence, for which treasonous communication the Earl of Oxford and others were executed in the same year; it was Margaret who sailed again for France in 1463 with her young son, where they set up a court in exile in her father's domains in Lorraine.

During this time Henry remained in Scotland or northern England, a figurehead giving no leadership to a cause that appeared to be in terminal decline. The defeats of Henry's northern supporters at Hedgeley Moor and Hexham in April and May 1464, at neither of which Henry was present, and the final fall of a number of Lancastrian castles in Northumberland ended the military threat to

Edward IV on English soil (Harlech Castle in north Wales held out until 1468). Edward was also able to nullify Margaret's diplomatic efforts by a series of truces with Scotland and France. Deprived of Scottish support, Henry spent the year after the defeat at Hexham moving between friendly houses in Lancashire, West Yorkshire and Westmorland, sheltered by a few remaining loyalists. He was eventually discovered, perhaps betrayed by the Tempest family, with whom he had been staying. After a brief flight he was captured in a forest known as Clitherwood, accompanied only by two chaplains and a young squire. He was brought to London on horseback, with his feet tied to the stirrups, on 24 June 1465. Henry's life was spared as a result of the fact that his son was at liberty: executing Henry would simply have transferred Lancastrian allegiances to a young man whose youth and vigour would have contrasted favourably with his passive, failed father.

Henry was imprisoned in the Tower for the next five years, albeit in comfortable enough circumstances. He was allowed five marks a week for his food and expenses, a level of expenditure of a wealthy knight or a lesser baron, and at one stage had twenty-two men in attendance on him. Some of these may have been guards, but their number also included William Kymberley, a priest, who celebrated Mass for him daily. Occasionally velvet cloth was supplied from the royal wardrobe to be made into gowns and doublets for Henry, but we know nothing of how he spent his time, whether he read books, wrote anything, or undertook physical exercise. He was allowed visitors; one chronicler stated that any man might come and see him by licence of his gaolers.[1] Such conditions rather suggest that Edward thought there was nothing to fear from Henry; perhaps, indeed, he may have considered that by allowing people to see Henry, word might spread of his mentally enfeebled state. Henry, meanwhile, appears to have accepted this fate with complete resignation.

In September 1470, the most spectacular reversal of fortune of Henry's entire life, his release after five years in prison and restoration or, as it is usually known, readeption (from the Latin formula for the reattainment of his royal power), owed nothing to his actions, and only a little to the actions of his queen and son. The true reason lay in the split in the Yorkist regime, between Edward IV and the man who was formerly his greatest supporter, Richard Neville, Earl of Warwick, in alliance with Edward's own brother the Duke of Clarence, and in the general unpopularity of Edward's rule. The first ten years of Edward's reign had seen ongoing disturbances in many parts of the country, no great improvement in law and order, and a continued slump in foreign trade; taken together, these conditions made ruling an exceptionally difficult task for Edward, added to which his heavy taxation for foreign wars which never happened made him look greedy and duplicitous.

In the spring of 1470 Warwick's final break with Edward saw the earl flee to France and, that July, agree on bended knee before Queen Margaret to resume his Lancastrian allegiance and attempt to put Henry – whom Warwick had helped depose a decade previously – back on the throne. Two months later Edward, in the face of an invading army led by Warwick and Clarence and deserted by most of his allies and supporters, was forced to flee abroad to the Low Countries. On 3 October 1470, Henry was led from captivity to resume his reign. One Lancastrian chronicler alleged that he was not 'worshipfully arrayed as a prince and not so cleanly kept', but this may just be hostile, anti-Yorkist comment as Edward had spent more money on Henry than might have been expected.[2] The same chronicler added that all his supporters and the greater part of the people were glad of Henry's resumption of power: perhaps memories of his shortcomings as a king had faded, obscured by Edward's own failings, or perhaps people were aware that Henry was unlikely to be more than a figurehead for Warwick, Queen Margaret or Prince Edward to rule through and thus his weaknesses would be mitigated by strong leadership.

On 13 October Henry was paraded through the streets in the company of the leading lords, the Duke of Clarence and the Earls of Warwick and Oxford, in a formal crown-wearing ceremony, but otherwise the restored king's part in the events of the next few months appears to have been nominal. He stayed in London for the entire period of the readeption, not stirring himself in government, not going to the coast to meet the expected fleet of his wife and son – who in the event did not appear until later – nor even accompanying the army that Warwick commanded that sought to crush Edward IV, newly returned from his exile in the Low Countries into Yorkshire, in March 1471. Indeed, so passive did Henry seem that the Burgundian chronicler Georges Chastellain wrote shortly afterwards that Henry had become 'a stuffed wool sack lifted by his ears, a shadow on the wall, bandied about as in a game of blind-man's buff, submissive and mute . . . like a crowned calf'.[3]

Margaret of Anjou's delay in returning to England was fatal to the Lancastrian cause. If both elements of the anti-Yorkist coalition – Warwick's faction and Margaret's Lancastrian loyalists – had been able to combine forces, then it is likely that Edward could not have overcome them, but without the queen's forces and with Warwick, inclined to be overly cautious, in command of the Lancastrian armies, the odds were rather more even than should have been the case. With only a few hundred men, Edward landed at Ravenspur in Yorkshire, and as he marched to York and then south he slowly gathered support. Even substantially outnumbering his opponents, Warwick could not be drawn from his stronghold at Coventry, and Edward marched on London.

Warwick's brother George Neville, Archbishop of York, the senior Lancastrian left in the capital, paraded Henry through the city in order to strengthen the will of the citizens to resist Edward IV's approaching army but, according to at least one chronicle account, it had the opposite effect. One chronicler used Henry's long blue gown, in which he constantly appeared in public 'as though he had no more to change with', as evidence of a shabby display in an age where kings were expected to be demonstrably magnificent and which, the chronicler argued, 'lost many [hearts] and won none or right few'.[4] He was, though, unduly harsh. The day of the procession, 11 April 1471, was

Maundy Thursday, on which it was traditional to wear blue, the royal colour of mourning. A German writing from London a few days later simply noted that Henry rode through the city 'to comfort the people', while another chronicler, more positive towards the Lancastrians, says that Henry's procession in fact achieved its morale-boosting aim, and that Edward IV was actually allowed into the city by a ruse.[5] However it was achieved, Edward entered the city, and took custody of Henry VI once more. Extraordinarily, there survives a credible report of the words exchanged between them. Henry said to Edward, 'My cousin of York, you are very welcome. I know that in your hands my life will not be in danger.' Edward replied that he was not to worry about anything, he would fare well.[6] The non-specific reply, however, clearly indicated that Edward did not want to commit to Henry's long-term well-being.

Edward kept Henry close to him. He was probably in Edward's camp on the morning of the Battle of Barnet, 14 April 1471, in which Edward, with a considerable amount of good fortune, defeated Warwick and his allies in a bloody encounter in which Warwick and his brother were killed. Afterwards, Henry was returned to the Tower of London while Edward then marched swiftly to deal with Queen Margaret and Prince Edward who, the same day as Barnet but too late to influence events there, had landed at Weymouth in Dorset. Marching north with the aim of joining Lancastrians in Wales, they were intercepted by Edward's forces on 4 May at the Gloucestershire town of Tewkesbury and Edward, without needing recourse to luck, emerged victorious again. Crucially, this time Queen

Margaret was captured; Prince Edward, then aged seventeen, was killed trying to flee the field.

With the death of Prince Edward at Tewkesbury, Henry VI was no longer of any use to the victorious Edward IV; indeed, his continued existence only served as a reminder of the previous decade of civil war. All accounts agree that he died during the night of 21 May, the same day that Edward returned to London in triumph. The official Yorkist account, that he died of pure displeasure, was not likely to have been believed at the time, and certainly has not been subsequently. Two chronicles, less official and written before or just after Henry's nephew, Henry Tudor, claimed the throne in 1485 and sought to blacken Richard III's name, claim that he was murdered. One, Warkworth's chronicle, noted that Richard, Duke of Gloucester and many others were present in the Tower that night, and was the precursor to the tradition eagerly picked up in Tudor times and enshrined in Shakespeare, that Gloucester committed the deed. However, not only was it highly unlikely that Gloucester actually committed the act, but also the decision to kill him must have been taken by the highest authority in the land, King Edward himself. It is with Edward that the final responsibility for Henry's death must rest.

We do not know how he was killed. In 1910, Henry's tomb in St George's Chapel, Windsor, was opened and the remains examined. His hair was brown, as could be seen from some still attached to the skull; in a rather sensationalist addition, it was claimed that one part of the surviving hair was darker, and apparently matted with blood. This is a dangerous assumption, made with the benefit of hindsight; a blow to the head would have been unsubtle and, given that the body was displayed in public outside St Paul's Cathedral the next day, perhaps unlikely. Henry's posthumous cult instead placed emphasis on him being stabbed with a dagger, which is rather more plausible. Warkworth claimed that the body bled on the pavement, and when taken to Blackfriars (the site of one of the great religious buildings in medieval London), again bled there. Not only is this medically unlikely, but this description is a literary trope regarding murder victims.

Henry was taken to Chertsey Abbey in Surrey to be buried, not perhaps as befitted a king, but with a level of expenditure that allowed for a certain ceremonial. Chertsey was not an appropriate burial site for a monarch: it was intended, presumably, to ensure his memory faded in this obscure abbey. If so, it failed. A cult to the king was already well established within two years of his death. A statue of him in York Minster was known to be venerated in 1473; in 1480 Edward IV attempted to stop those 'in going of Pilgrimage to King Henry' at Chertsey.[7] In 1484 Richard III had Henry moved to Windsor to lie opposite his old rival Edward IV, in part so he could benefit from the popular veneration of Henry as a saint.

After the accession of Henry's nephew, Henry Tudor, in 1485 more official efforts were made to persuade the papacy of his saintliness, and papal agents collected books filled with Henry's alleged miracles in 1494 and 1504; 368 miracles were ascribed to Henry's agency, the earliest dating from 1481. Badges were made of Henry for pilgrims to buy – nearly four hundred have been found, mostly but not exclusively in southern England. Rood screens were painted, occasional statues were made, and the church of Caversham in Berkshire contained a relic purporting to be the dagger with which Henry had been murdered. The cult of Henry VI was flourishing, and remained buoyant until the English Reformation.

It is hard not to feel sympathy for Henry VI. To be a king in fifteenth-century England when kingship was a difficult task taxed able men to the limit. Henry, however, was not an able king. He was a manifestly decent man placed by accident of birth in a role to which he was utterly unsuited; a man of piety when he needed to be a man of policy; a man uninterested in the business of kingship when kingship meant business; a man of peace whose inheritance was foreign conflict and whose rule bred civil war. The veneration in which he was held after his death was a testament to the fact that his subjects understood his virtues, but had nevertheless suffered from his failings. His reign saw a catalogue of disasters, including the loss of newly conquered Normandy, long-held Gascony, increasing factionalism, and then outright civil war in England. Both rich and poor suffered, and the Wars of the Roses finally claimed Henry's life and ended his dynasty.

Notes

ABBREVIATIONS

PL   *The Paston Letters*, ed. J. Gairdner (6 vols, London: Chatto and Windus, 1904)

PPC   *Proceedings and Ordinances of the Privy Council*, ed. N. H. Nicolas (7 vols, London: Record Commission, 1834–7)

PROME   *Parliament Rolls of Medieval England 1275–1504* (17 vols, Woodbridge/London: The Boydell Press/The National Archives, 2005)

TNA   The National Archives, Kew, London

INTRODUCTION:
THE ENIGMA OF HENRY VI

1. William Shakespeare, *Henry V*, Epilogue.
2. Sir John Fortescue, *The Governance of England*, ed. C. Plummer (Oxford: Clarendon Press, 1885), p. 121.
3. K. B. McFarlane, *The Nobility of Later Medieval England* (Oxford: Clarendon Press, 1973), p. 284.
4. R. A. Griffiths, *The Reign of Henry VI* (London: Benn, 1981), p. xxiv.
5. Particularly M. Hicks, *The Wars of the Roses* (London and New Haven: Yale University Press, 2010) and D. Grummitt, *Henry VI* (Abingdon: Routledge, 2015).
6. C. Harper-Bill, *The Pre-Reformation Church in England, 1400–1530* (London: Longman, 1989), p. 10.

I. BEHIND THE FACADE: HENRY'S
CHARACTER AND CAPABILITY

1. *Foedera, Conventiones, Litterae . . . et Acta Publica*, ed. T. Rymer (20 vols, London: J. Tonson, 1704–35), X, p. 399.
2. *Calendar of Patent Rolls, 1452–61*, p. 247.
3. *PPC*, IV, pp. 135–6.

4. Ibid., pp. 287-9.

5. *PROME*, XII, ed. A. Curry and R. Horrox, p. 518.

6. Titus Livius Frulovisi's *Vita Henrici Quinti* (*Life of Henry V*), a work written for Henry's youngest brother, Humphrey, Duke of Gloucester, and perhaps based on the latter's reminiscences.

7. Written by John Lydgate, the Prior of Hatfield Regis, a prolific writer and poet, extensively patronized by the Lancastrian kings and court.

8. *Four English Political Tracts of the Later Middle Ages*, ed. J. P. Genet (London: Camden Society, 4th series, 18, 1977), pp. 40-173.

9. John Blacman, *Henry VI*, ed. M. R. James (Cambridge: Cambridge University Press, 1955), p. 5.

10. An account of Henry's visit is printed in *Monasticism in Late Medieval England, c.1300-1535*, ed. M. Heale (Manchester: Manchester University Press, 2009), pp. 188-93.

11. R. A. Griffiths, 'The Minority of Henry VI, King of England and of France', in *The Royal Minorities of Medieval and Early Modern England*, ed. C. Beem (New York, Basingstoke: Palgrave Macmillan, 2008), p. 176.

12. A contemporary witness to his canonization proceedings, quoted in G. Duby, *France in the Middle Ages, 987-1460*, trans. J. Vale (Oxford: Blackwell, 1991), p. 258.

13. Blacman, *Henry VI*, pp. 4, 5, 7.

14. The original Latin is printed in *Piero da Monte, ein Gelehrter und Päpstlicher Beamter des 15. Jahrhunderts, seine Briefsammlung*, ed. Johannes Haller (Deutsches Historisches Institut, 19, Rome, 1941), pp. 43-5, summarized in A. N. E. D. Schofield, 'England, the Pope and the Council of Basel, 1435-1449', *Church History*, 33 (1964), p. 259 and n. 61.

15. T. Hoccleve, *The Regement of Princes*, ed. F. J. Furnivall (London: K. Paul, Trench, Trübner & Co., 1897), pp. 120, 125, 131, 137 (quote).

16. *Registra Quorundam Abbatum Monasterii Sancti Albani*, ed. H. T. Riley (2 vols, Rolls Series, London: Longman, 1872-3), I, p. 415. John Capgrave, writing around 1450, noted the reverence with which he adored the sign of the cross whenever he met his priests, echoing the Abbot of Bury St Edmunds's description in 1433, and also referenced his abstention from feasting and drunkenness. A well-connected German in London, Hans Winter, commenting on the economic and diplomatic woes of 1449, did not consider the king to blame as he 'is very young and inexperienced and watched over as a Carthusian [monk]': quoted in M. M. Postan, 'The Economic and Political Relations of England and the Hanse from 1400-1475', in *Studies in English Trade in the Fifteenth Century*, ed. E. Power and M. M. Postan (London: Routledge, 1933), pp. 376-7, n. 60, and see also n. 63.

17. J. Rous, *Historia Regum Angliae*, ed. T. Hearne (Oxford: J. Fletcher, 1745), p. 210.

18. TNA, KB 9/260, no. 85.

19. *Historical Manuscript Commission, Fifth Report* (London: HMSO, 1876), p. 455a, citing Canterbury Cathedral Archives, M. 238, dating from 1448.

20. Blacman, *Henry VI*, p. 7.

21. Ibid, p. 8.

22. *Piero da Monte*, ed. Haller, p. 44; Matthew 5:28.

23. *English Historical Documents IV (1327-1485)*, ed. A. R. Myers (London: Eyre and Spottiswoode, 1969), p. 257.

24. *Calendar of State Papers: Milan, I, 1385–1618* (London: HMSO, 1912), pp. 18–19.

25. British Library, London, Add. MS 38174, ff. 19v–20r, 36v–37r, printed in *The Antiquarian Repertory*, ed. F. Grose (4 vols, London: Jeffery, 1807–9), I, p. 313 (for Henry and Margaret), p. 330 (Edward and Elizabeth).

26. K. E. Selway, 'The Role of Eton College and King's College, Cambridge, in the Polity of the Lancastrian Monarchy' (unpublished Oxford D.Phil. thesis, 1993), p. 207.

27. TNA, C81/1451, no. 12.

28. R. Willis and J. W. Clark, *Architectural History of the University of Cambridge* (3 vols, Cambridge: Cambridge University Press, 1886), I, p. 353.

29. Ibid., p. 380.

30. *Official Correspondence of Thomas Bekynton*, ed. G. Williams (2 vols, Rolls Series, London: Longman, 56, 1872), I, p. 175.

31. *PROME*, XII, ed. Curry and Horrox, p. 187.

32. Fortescue, *Governance of England*, p. 125.

33. Blacman, *Henry VI*, p. 14.

34. TNA, E101/409/2, ff. 31–4.

35. TNA, E101/409/12, ff. 53–5.

36. *Letters and Papers Illustrative of the Wars of the English in France during the Reign of Henry VI*, ed. J. Stevenson (2 vols in 3, Rolls Series, London: Longman, 1861–4), I, p. 103.

37. A. R. Myers, *The Household of Edward IV: The Black Book and the Ordinance of 1478* (Manchester: Manchester University Press, 1959), p. 5.

38. *Liber Regie Capelle*, ed. W. Ullmann (London: Henry Bradshaw Society, 92, 1961).

39. D. Starkey, 'Henry VI's Old Blue Gown: The English Court under the Lancastrians and Yorkists', *The Court Historian*, 4 (1999), pp. 1–28; *The Antiquarian Repertory*, ed. Grose, I, pp. 296–341.

40. *Calendar of Fine Rolls, 1437–45*, p. 34.

41. *PPC*, V, pp. 88–9.

42. K. J. Lewis, *Kingship and Masculinity in Late Medieval England* (Abingdon: Routledge, 2013), p. 166.

43. TNA, C81/1450, no. 8.

44. TNA, C81/1447, no. 27.

45. Blacman, *Henry VI*, pp. 15–16.

46. J. L. Watts, *Henry VI and the Politics of Kingship* (Cambridge: Cambridge University Press, 1996), Chapters 5 and 6.

47. *PROME*, X, ed. Curry, p. 326.

48. *The First English Life of King Henry the Fifth*, ed. C. L. Kingsford (Oxford: Clarendon Press, 1911), p. 7.

49. C. A. F. Meekings, 'Thomas Kerver's Case', *English Historical Review*, 90 (1975), p. 332.

50. Kent History and Library Centre, Maidstone, DRb/A/r/1/10, f. 65v–66r. I am very grateful to Dr Maureen Jurkowski for this reference. A nearly identical letter was sent to the Bishop of Hereford a week earlier: *Registrum Thome Spofford, Episcopi Herefordensis*, ed. A. T. Bannister (London: Canterbury and York Society, 1919), pp. 252–4.

51. C. D. Ross, *The Wars of the Roses* (London: Thames and Hudson, 1976), p. 118.

2. POLICY AND PROFLIGACY, 1436–1453

1. Both letters are British Library, Add. MS 14848, f. 191v.
2. *Wars of the English in France*, ed. Stevenson, II, ii, p. 452.
3. Ibid., I, pp. 111–12, 124.
4. Ibid., II, ii, pp. 639–40.
5. *Three Fifteenth-Century Chronicles*, ed. J. Gairdner (London: Camden Society, new series, 28, 1880), p. 96.
6. Joseph A. Nigota, 'Fiennes, James, first Baron Saye and Sele (*c.*1390–1450)', in *Oxford Dictionary of National Biography* (Oxford University Press, 2004); online edn, Jan. 2008 [http://www.oxforddnb.com/view/article/9411, accessed 28 Sept. 2015].
7. *Three Fifteenth-Century Chronicles*, ed. Gairdner, p. 96.
8. Watts, *Henry VI and the Politics of Kingship*, p. 199, n. 331.
9. 'Gregory's Chronicle', in *Historical Collections of a London Citizen* (London: Camden Society, new series, 17, 1876), p. 197.
10. B. Wolffe, *Henry VI* (London and New Haven: Yale University Press, 1981), p. 238.

3. COLLAPSE AND CATASTROPHE, 1453–1461

1. *Incerti Auctoris Chronicon Angliae*, ed. J. A. Giles (London: D. Nutt, 1848), pp. 43–4.
2. *PL*, II, pp. 295–6. John Stodeley, writing from London on 19 January 1454.
3. *PROME*, XII, ed. Curry and Horrox, p. 259.
4. Quoted in B. Clarke, *Mental Disorder in Earlier Britain* (Cardiff: University of Wales Press, 1975), p. 188.
5. *PL*, III, pp. 2–3. William Paston to John Paston, 6 September 1454. A second bishop, William Grey, also did his fealty to the king around this time as well, as noted in the same letter.
6. *PL*, III, p. 13. Edmund Clere to John Paston, 9 January 1455.
7. R. L. Storey, *The End of the House of Lancaster* (London: Barrie and Rockliff, 1966), p. 159.
8. Average figure derived from the subseries of 'signed bills and other direct warrants' among the Warrants for the Great Seal only, TNA, C81/1464, compared to C81/1437–41, 1451–4.
9. *Calendar of State Papers: Milan*, I, p. 16.
10. 'Benet's Chronicle', ed. G. L. Harriss and M. A. Harriss, in *Camden Miscellany XXIV* (London: Camden Society, 4th series, 9, 1972), pp. 213–14.
11. TNA, KB 9/287, no. 53.
12. *PL*, III, p. 50.
13. *PROME*, XII, ed. Curry and Horrox, pp. 347, 349.
14. Ibid., p. 454.
15. Griffiths, *Reign of Henry VI*, p. 775; Hicks, *Wars of the Roses*, p. 152.

16. G. Beaucourt, *Histoire de Charles VII* (6 vols, Paris: Société Bibliographique, 1881–91), VI, p. 137; *The Coventry Leet Book*, ed. M. D. Harris (London: Early English Text Society, old series 134–5, 138, 146, 1907–13), pts I, II, p. 301.

17. Ibid., p. 299.

18. A. P. Stanley, *Historical Memorials of Westminster Abbey* (3rd edn, London: J. Murray, 1869), p. 607.

19. Ibid., p. 601.

20. *Ingulph's Chronicle of the Abbey of Croyland with the Continuations by Peter of Blois and Anonymous Writers*, ed. H. T. Riley (London: H. G. Bohn, 1854), p. 420.

21. Thomas Gascoigne, *Loci e Libro Veritatum*, ed. J. E. Thorold Rogers (Oxford: Clarendon Press, 1881), p. 204.

22. *The Brut, or the Chronicles of England*, ed. F. W. D. Brie (London: Early English Text Society, 136, 1908), II, p. 527.

23. *Ingulph's Chronicle of the Abbey of Croyland*, ed. Riley, p. 424.

24. *Calendar of State Papers: Milan*, I, p. 61.

25. Quoted in C. Head, 'Pope Pius II and the Wars of the Roses', *Archivium Historiae Pontificiae*, 8 (1970), p. 145.

26. Michael Hicks has recently argued this case forcibly in his *Wars of the Roses*, Chapters 8 and 9, on which this paragraph is based.

27. TNA, C81/1468, no. 21 (dated 4 March 1458).

28. As John Watts has argued in his *Henry VI and the Politics of Kingship*.

29. TNA, C81/1371, no. 50.

30. TNA, C81/1465–1476, no. 54. A few do not bear the sign manual, but are otherwise authorized by the signet or other immediate action. However, for the purposes of the following discussion, they will be treated as being directly authorized by the king.

31. *PL*, III, p. 75. John Bocking to Sir John Fastolf, 9 February 1456.

32. 'Benet's Chronicle', ed. Harriss and Harriss, p. 209.

CONCLUSION:
DEATH AND AFTERLIFE

1. *A Chronicle of the First Thirteen Years of the Reign of Edward IV by John Warkworth*, ed. J. O. Halliwell (London: Camden Society, old series, 10, 1839), p. 6.

2. Ibid., p. 11.

3. Chastellain, quoted in J. H. Ramsay, *Lancaster and York* (2 vols, Oxford: Clarendon Press, 1892), II, p. 363.

4. *The Great Chronicle of London*, ed. A. H. Thomas and I. D. Thornley (London: Jones, 1938), p. 215.

5. H. Kleineke, 'Gerhard von Wesel's Newsletter from England, 17 April 1471', *The Ricardian*, 16 (2006), p. 7; *Warkworth's Chronicle*, ed. Halliwell, p. 15.

6. *Anchiennes Cronicques D'Engleterre Par Jehan de Wavrin*, ed. M. Dupont (3 vols, Paris: 1858–63), III, p. 211.

7. *The Fabric Rolls of York Minster*, ed. J. Raine (Durham: Surtees Society, 35, 1859), p. 83; *Acts of Court of the Mercers' Company, 1453–1527*, ed. L. Lyell (Cambridge: Cambridge University Press, 1936), p. 139.

Further Reading

There are three full-length studies of Henry and his reign published in the 1980s and 1990s which have formed the basis of modern scholarship. Bertram Wolffe, *Henry VI* (London and New Haven: Yale University Press, 1981), although clear and concise, is perhaps the least convincing, portraying Henry as active, vindictive and responsible for the disasters of his reign. R. A. Griffiths's monumental *The Reign of Henry VI* (London: Benn, 1981) is both a formidable work of scholarship, based on exhaustive research, and the most influential work on Henry, showing him as an active, well-meaning yet ultimately disastrous king. J. L. Watts, *Henry VI and the Politics of Kingship* (Cambridge: Cambridge University Press, 1996) offers a radical reinterpretation portraying Henry as a nonentity, a figurehead throughout his reign, and placing a great deal of emphasis on the political culture of the period in explaining events.

Of more recent studies K. J. Lewis, *Kingship and Masculinity in Late Medieval England* (Abingdon: Routledge, 2013) views Henry through the prism of gender, producing a different but not entirely convincing interpretation. M. A. Hicks, *The Wars of the Roses* (London and New Haven: Yale University Press, 2010) has argued for a greater level of Henry's involvement in ruling than previously accepted, particularly after 1455. David Grummitt's *Henry VI* (Abingdon: Routledge, 2015) takes a similar view of Henry to Ralph Griffiths, but places him within a context of political culture labelled 'Lancastrianism' that is interpreted very widely. J. W. McKenna, 'Piety and Propaganda: The Cult of King Henry VI', in *Chaucer and Middle English Studies*, ed. B. Rowland (London: Allen and Unwin, 1974), pp. 72–88, is an excellent study of Henry's afterlife.

There are biographies of other leading figures of the period, such as Queen Margaret by H. E. Maurer, *Margaret of Anjou: Queenship and Power in Late Medieval England* (Woodbridge: Boydell Press, 2003), Richard of York by P. A. Johnson, *Duke Richard of York* (Oxford: Clarendon Press, 1988) and Warwick the Kingmaker by M. A. Hicks, *Warwick the Kingmaker* (Oxford: Blackwell, 1998) and A. J. Pollard, *Warwick the Kingmaker: Politics, Power and Fame* (London: Hambledon Continuum, 2007). There is a good study of Henry's father, Henry V, by C. T. Allmand, *Henry V* (London and New Haven: Yale University Press, 1997, new edition). For the reign of Henry's successor, see C. D. Ross, *Edward IV* (London and New Haven: Yale University Press, 1997, new edition) and H. Kleineke, *Edward IV* (London: Routledge, 2009).

Certain events and themes discussed in this book can be explored further. The best single discussion of the Lancastrian court is D. Starkey, 'Henry VI's Old Blue Gown: The English Court under the Lancastrians and Yorkists', *The Court Historian*, 4 (1999), pp. 1–28. The popular uprising known as Cade's Revolt has been exhaustively studied by I. M. W. Harvey, *Jack Cade's Rebellion of 1450* (Oxford: Clarendon Press, 1991). Different areas of England's French possessions are discussed at length in C. T. Allmand, *Lancastrian Normandy, 1415–1450: The History of a Medieval Occupation* (Oxford: Clarendon Press, 1983) and M. G. A. Vale, *English Gascony, 1399–1453: A Study of War, Government and Politics During the Later Stages of the Hundred Years' War* (Oxford: Oxford University Press, 1970). For the best general background to England, its people, institutions and events, see G. L. Harriss, *Shaping the Nation: England 1360–1461* (Oxford: Clarendon Press, 2005).

The most important single contemporary text on Henry is John Blacman's *Henry VI*, ed. M. R. James (Cambridge: Cambridge University Press, 1955). Selections from contemporary chronicles and administrative records can be found in *Henry VI, Margaret of Anjou and the Wars of the Roses: A Source Book* (Stroud: Sutton, 2000) and *Edward IV: A Source Book* (Stroud: Sutton, 1999) both edited by Keith Dockray.

Picture Credits

1. Descent of crown of England and France. BL Royal 15 E VI, f. 3 (© The British Library Board)

2. Lydgate's life of St Edmund, picture of boy king praying. BL Harley MS 2278, f. 4v (© The British Library Board)

3. Henry's vernacular bible. MS Bodley 277 f. 375r (The Bodleian Library, University of Oxford)

4. Illuminated miniature of Henry in the foundation charter of King's College, Cambridge, 1441, MS Mun. KC/18/NI (King's College Library, Cambridge). Archives Centre, King's College Cambridge, KC/18 (© DIAMM; by kind permission of DIAMM, and the Provost and Fellows of King's College)

5. Chapel, King's College, Cambridge (© John Baran/Alamy Stock Photo); Eton Chapel (© NSP-RF/Alamy Stock Photo)

6. Pilgrim badge of Henry VI (Museum of London)

7. The only known example of Henry's signature, as opposed to sign manual or with a wooden stamp. The National Archives (TNA), E28/57, no. 28 (National Archives)

8. Variations in signs manual in the later 1450s: Top left – TNA, C81/1468, no. 26; Top right – C81/1468, no. 14; Bottom – C81/1473, no. 65 (National Archives)

9. TNA, C81/1447, no. 39, autograph annotation on grant to Bridlington priory (National Archives)

10. Screen painting of Henry VI in the chancel of the south chapel of Barton Turf, Norfolk (© ASP Religion/Alamy Stock Photo)

Acknowledgements

Friends and family have, as always, contributed in diverse ways, and thanks are owed to them, and in particular to Anna, for her love and support, and my children Chloe and Daniel, as sources of both love and diversion.

I am very grateful to Maureen Jurkowski, Hannes Kleineke and Simon Payling for references and suggestions. Tom Penn, both as a careful editor and as a historian with whom I discussed Henry on many occasions, has been a constant source of advice and support.

Lastly, there are three distinguished fifteenth-century historians who have directly or indirectly influenced this work, and to whom I owe a great deal. Rowena Archer, who shaped me as a historian, perhaps more than she realizes. John Watts, whose view on Henry VI is different from my own, and who will, I am sure, find fault in these pages, but with whom I first studied Henry VI in depth as an undergraduate and immensely enjoyed the process; he was also more tolerant of undergraduate pretensions to knowledge than he needed to be. Ralph Griffiths read this book in draft; his advice improved the text and forced me to reconsider many elements of Henry's life. This study owes a great deal to his work on Henry VI. Needless to say, any errors remain my own.

Index

Penguin Monarchs

THE HOUSES OF WESSEX AND DENMARK

Athelstan*	Tom Holland
Aethelred the Unready	Richard Abels
Cnut	Ryan Lavelle
Edward the Confessor	David Woodman

THE HOUSES OF NORMANDY, BLOIS AND ANJOU

William I*	Marc Morris
William II*	John Gillingham
Henry I	Edmund King
Stephen*	Carl Watkins
Henry II*	Richard Barber
Richard I*	Thomas Asbridge
John	Nicholas Vincent

THE HOUSE OF PLANTAGENET

Henry III*	Stephen Church
Edward I*	Andy King
Edward II*	Christopher Given-Wilson
Edward III*	Jonathan Sumption
Richard II*	Laura Ashe

THE HOUSES OF LANCASTER AND YORK

Henry IV	Catherine Nall
Henry V*	Anne Curry
Henry VI*	James Ross
Edward IV*	A. J. Pollard
Edward V	Thomas Penn
Richard III	Rosemary Horrox

* Now in paperback

THE HOUSE OF TUDOR

Henry VII — Sean Cunningham
Henry VIII* — John Guy
Edward VI* — Stephen Alford
Mary I* — John Edwards
Elizabeth I* — Helen Castor

THE HOUSE OF STUART

James I* — Thomas Cogswell
Charles I* — Mark Kishlansky
[Cromwell* — David Horspool]
Charles II* — Clare Jackson
James II* — David Womersley
William III & Mary II* — Jonathan Keates
Anne — Richard Hewlings

THE HOUSE OF HANOVER

George I* — Tim Blanning
George II — Norman Davies
George III — Amanda Foreman
George IV — Stella Tillyard
William IV* — Roger Knight
Victoria* — Jane Ridley

THE HOUSES OF SAXE-COBURG & GOTHA AND WINDSOR

Edward VII* — Richard Davenport-Hines
George V* — David Cannadine
Edward VIII* — Piers Brendon
George VI* — Philip Ziegler
Elizabeth II* — Douglas Hurd

* Now in paperback

ALLEN LANE
an imprint of
PENGUIN BOOKS

Also Published

Stephen Kotkin, *Stalin, Vol. II: Waiting for Hitler, 1928-1941*

Lindsey Fitzharris, *The Butchering Art: Joseph Lister's Quest to Transform the Grisly World of Victorian Medicine*

Serhii Plokhy, *Lost Kingdom: A History of Russian Nationalism from Ivan the Great to Vladimir Putin*

Mark Mazower, *What You Did Not Tell: A Russian Past and the Journey Home*

Lawrence Freedman, *The Future of War: A History*

Niall Ferguson, *The Square and the Tower: Networks, Hierarchies and the Struggle for Global Power*

Matthew Walker, *Why We Sleep: The New Science of Sleep and Dreams*

Edward O. Wilson, *The Origins of Creativity*

John Bradshaw, *The Animals Among Us: The New Science of Anthropology*

David Cannadine, *Victorious Century: The United Kingdom, 1800-1906*

Leonard Susskind and Art Friedman, *Special Relativity and Classical Field Theory*

Maria Alyokhina, *Riot Days*

Oona A. Hathaway and Scott J. Shapiro, *The Internationalists: And Their Plan to Outlaw War*

Chris Renwick, *Bread for All: The Origins of the Welfare State*

Anne Applebaum, *Red Famine: Stalin's War on Ukraine*

Richard McGregor, *Asia's Reckoning: The Struggle for Global Dominance*

Chris Kraus, *After Kathy Acker: A Biography*

Clair Wills, *Lovers and Strangers: An Immigrant History of Post-War Britain*

Odd Arne Westad, *The Cold War: A World History*

Max Tegmark, *Life 3.0: Being Human in the Age of Artificial Intelligence*

Jonathan Losos, *Improbable Destinies: How Predictable is Evolution?*

Chris D. Thomas, *Inheritors of the Earth: How Nature Is Thriving in an Age of Extinction*

Chris Patten, *First Confession: A Sort of Memoir*

James Delbourgo, *Collecting the World: The Life and Curiosity of Hans Sloane*

Naomi Klein, *No Is Not Enough: Defeating the New Shock Politics*

Ulrich Raulff, *Farewell to the Horse: The Final Century of Our Relationship*

Slavoj Žižek, *The Courage of Hopelessness: Chronicles of a Year of Acting Dangerously*

Patricia Lockwood, *Priestdaddy: A Memoir*

Ian Johnson, *The Souls of China: The Return of Religion After Mao*

Stephen Alford, *London's Triumph: Merchant Adventurers and the Tudor City*

Hugo Mercier and Dan Sperber, *The Enigma of Reason: A New Theory of Human Understanding*

Stuart Hall, *Familiar Stranger: A Life Between Two Islands*

Allen Ginsberg, *The Best Minds of My Generation: A Literary History of the Beats*

Sayeeda Warsi, *The Enemy Within: A Tale of Muslim Britain*

Alexander Betts and Paul Collier, *Refuge: Transforming a Broken Refugee System*

Robert Bickers, *Out of China: How the Chinese Ended the Era of Western Domination*

Erica Benner, *Be Like the Fox: Machiavelli's Lifelong Quest for Freedom*

William D. Cohan, *Why Wall Street Matters*

David Horspool, *Oliver Cromwell: The Protector*

Daniel C. Dennett, *From Bacteria to Bach and Back: The Evolution of Minds*

Derek Thompson, *Hit Makers: How Things Become Popular*

Harriet Harman, *A Woman's Work*

Wendell Berry, *The World-Ending Fire: The Essential Wendell Berry*

Daniel Levin, *Nothing but a Circus: Misadventures among the Powerful*

Stephen Church, *Henry III: A Simple and God-Fearing King*

Pankaj Mishra, *Age of Anger: A History of the Present*

Graeme Wood, *The Way of the Strangers: Encounters with the Islamic State*

Michael Lewis, *The Undoing Project: A Friendship that Changed the World*

John Romer, *A History of Ancient Egypt, Volume 2: From the Great Pyramid to the Fall of the Middle Kingdom*

Andy King, *Edward I: A New King Arthur?*

Thomas L. Friedman, *Thank You for Being Late: An Optimist's Guide to Thriving in the Age of Accelerations*

John Edwards, *Mary I: The Daughter of Time*

Grayson Perry, *The Descent of Man*

Deyan Sudjic, *The Language of Cities*

Norman Ohler, *Blitzed: Drugs in Nazi Germany*

Carlo Rovelli, *Reality Is Not What It Seems: The Journey to Quantum Gravity*

Catherine Merridale, *Lenin on the Train*

Susan Greenfield, *A Day in the Life of the Brain: The Neuroscience of Consciousness from Dawn Till Dusk*

Christopher Given-Wilson, *Edward II: The Terrors of Kingship*

Emma Jane Kirby, *The Optician of Lampedusa*

Minoo Dinshaw, *Outlandish Knight: The Byzantine Life of Steven Runciman*

Candice Millard, *Hero of the Empire: The Making of Winston Churchill*

Christopher de Hamel, *Meetings with Remarkable Manuscripts*

Brian Cox and Jeff Forshaw, *Universal: A Guide to the Cosmos*

Ryan Avent, *The Wealth of Humans: Work and Its Absence in the Twenty-first Century*

Jodie Archer and Matthew L. Jockers, *The Bestseller Code*

Cathy O'Neil, *Weapons of Math Destruction: How Big Data Increases Inequality and Threatens Democracy*

Peter Wadhams, *A Farewell to Ice: A Report from the Arctic*

Richard J. Evans, *The Pursuit of Power: Europe, 1815-1914*

Anthony Gottlieb, *The Dream of Enlightenment: The Rise of Modern Philosophy*

Marc Morris, *William I: England's Conqueror*

Gareth Stedman Jones, *Karl Marx: Greatness and Illusion*

J.C.H. King, *Blood and Land: The Story of Native North America*

Robert Gerwarth, *The Vanquished: Why the First World War Failed to End, 1917-1923*

Joseph Stiglitz, *The Euro: And Its Threat to Europe*

John Bradshaw and Sarah Ellis, *The Trainable Cat: How to Make Life Happier for You and Your Cat*

A J Pollard, *Edward IV: The Summer King*

Erri de Luca, *The Day Before Happiness*

Diarmaid MacCulloch, *All Things Made New: Writings on the Reformation*

Daniel Beer, *The House of the Dead: Siberian Exile Under the Tsars*

Tom Holland, *Athelstan: The Making of England*

Christopher Goscha, *The Penguin History of Modern Vietnam*

Mark Singer, *Trump and Me*

Roger Scruton, *The Ring of Truth: The Wisdom of Wagner's Ring of the Nibelung*

Ruchir Sharma, *The Rise and Fall of Nations: Ten Rules of Change in the Post-Crisis World*

Jonathan Sumption, *Edward III: A Heroic Failure*

Daniel Todman, *Britain's War: Into Battle, 1937-1941*

Dacher Keltner, *The Power Paradox: How We Gain and Lose Influence*

Tom Gash, *Criminal: The Truth About Why People Do Bad Things*

Brendan Simms, *Britain's Europe: A Thousand Years of Conflict and Cooperation*

Slavoj Žižek, *Against the Double Blackmail: Refugees, Terror, and Other Troubles with the Neighbours*

Lynsey Hanley, *Respectable: The Experience of Class*

Piers Brendon, *Edward VIII: The Uncrowned King*

Matthew Desmond, *Evicted: Poverty and Profit in the American City*

T.M. Devine, *Independence or Union: Scotland's Past and Scotland's Present*

Seamus Murphy, *The Republic*

Jerry Brotton, *This Orient Isle: Elizabethan England and the Islamic World*

Srinath Raghavan, *India's War: The Making of Modern South Asia, 1939-1945*

Clare Jackson, *Charles II: The Star King*

Nandan Nilekani and Viral Shah, *Rebooting India: Realizing a Billion Aspirations*

Sunil Khilnani, *Incarnations: India in 50 Lives*

Helen Pearson, *The Life Project: The Extraordinary Story of Our Ordinary Lives*

Ben Ratliff, *Every Song Ever: Twenty Ways to Listen to Music Now*

Richard Davenport-Hines, *Edward VII: The Cosmopolitan King*

Peter H. Wilson, *The Holy Roman Empire: A Thousand Years of Europe's History*

Todd Rose, *The End of Average: How to Succeed in a World that Values Sameness*

Frank Trentmann, *Empire of Things: How We Became a World of Consumers, from the Fifteenth Century to the Twenty-First*

Laura Ashe, *Richard II: A Brittle Glory*

John Donvan and Caren Zucker, *In a Different Key: The Story of Autism*

Jack Shenker, *The Egyptians: A Radical Story*

Tim Judah, *In Wartime: Stories from Ukraine*

Serhii Plokhy, *The Gates of Europe: A History of Ukraine*

Robin Lane Fox, *Augustine: Conversions and Confessions*

Peter Hennessy and James Jinks, *The Silent Deep: The Royal Navy Submarine Service Since 1945*

Sean McMeekin, *The Ottoman Endgame: War, Revolution and the Making of the Modern Middle East, 1908–1923*

Charles Moore, *Margaret Thatcher: The Authorized Biography, Volume Two: Everything She Wants*

Dominic Sandbrook, *The Great British Dream Factory: The Strange History of Our National Imagination*

Larissa MacFarquhar, *Strangers Drowning: Voyages to the Brink of Moral Extremity*

Niall Ferguson, *Kissinger: 1923-1968: The Idealist*

Carlo Rovelli, *Seven Brief Lessons on Physics*

Tim Blanning, *Frederick the Great: King of Prussia*

Ian Kershaw, *To Hell and Back: Europe, 1914–1949*

Pedro Domingos, *The Master Algorithm: How the Quest for the Ultimate Learning Machine Will Remake Our World*

David Wootton, *The Invention of Science: A New History of the Scientific Revolution*